745.59412 Search   9/20
Search Press Studio
Quick and easy Christmas
100 gifts & decorations

Quick and Easy
CHRISTMAS

Quick and Easy
CHRISTMAS

100 gifts & decorations to make for the festive season

Search Press

First published in 2020

Search Press Limited
Wellwood, North Farm Road,
Tunbridge Wells, Kent TN2 3DR

Previously published in 2016 as *100 Little Christmas Gifts to Make* using material from a number of books in the *Twenty to Make* series published by Search Press. See page 240 for a full list.

Text copyright © Kate Haxell, Susanna Wallis, Alistair Macdonald, Corinne Lapierre, Michael Powell, Carolyn Forster, Alex McQuade, Myra Hutton, Ann Cox, Jayne Schofield, Michelle Powell, Sara Naumann, Diane Boden, Louise Crosbie, Paper Panda, Susan Penny, Val Pierce, Susie Johns, Sue Stratford, Monica Russel, Susan A. Cordes, Lee Ann Garrett, Amanda Walker, Stephanie Burnham, Michelle Bungay, Helen Birmingham, Marrianne Mercer, Sandy Griffiths, Pam Leach, Carolyn Schulz, Natalia Colman, Val Pierce, Jan Ollis, May Corfield, Anna Nikipirowicz, Frances McNaughton, Lisa Slatter, Georgie Godbold, Charlotte Stowell, Birdy Heywood, Karen Walker, frechverlag GmbH (Stuttgart, Germany) 2016

Photographs by Paul Bricknell, Debbie Patterson, Vanessa Davies, Laura Forrester, Roddy Paine, Fiona Murray, Ruth Jenkinson, Simon Pask, Mark Winwood, Rebecca Warwick, Angela Spain, Ivan Naudé

Photographs and design copyright
© Search Press Ltd 2016

ISBN: 978-1-78221-793-0

The Publishers and author can accept no responsibility for any consequences arising from the information, advice or instructions given in this publication.

Suppliers
If you have difficulty in obtaining any of the materials and equipment mentioned in this book, then please visit the Search Press website for details of suppliers:
www.searchpress.com

CONTENTS

Flowery Bunting, page 20

Pompom Cupcakes, page 22

Felt Winter Owl, page 24

Scottie Dog Brooch page 26

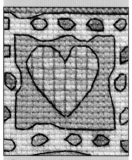
Cross Stitch Heart, page 28

Jelly Roll Bag, page 30

Pompom Santa, page 32

Daisy Brooch, page 34

Christmas Bunting,
page 36

Feltie Mouse, page 38

Felt Duck Brooch,
page 40

Fur Scatter Pillow,
page 42

Needlepoint Hen,
page 44

Silk Ribbon Poinsettia,
page 46

Christmas Tea Light,
page 48

Felt Place Setting,
page 50

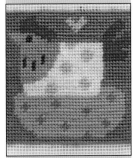

Heart Brooch,
page 52

Jelly Roll Pillow,
page 54

Pompom Card Pegs,
page 56

Fabric Button Flower,
page 58

Needlepoint Snowman,
page 60

Christmas Tree
Papercut, page 64

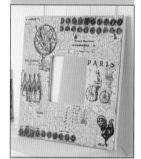

Bobble Scarf, page 98

Knitted Pear, page 100

Penguin Boot Cuffs, page 102

Christmas Holly Cake, page 104

Crystal Phone Sock, page 106

Pumpkin, page 108

Stripes Tea Cosy, page 110

Periwinkle, page 112

Bow Beanie, page 114

Berry Bootees, page 116

Wave Headband, page 118

Christmas Tree, page 120

Heart Mug Hug, page 122

Fair Isle Wrist Warmers,
page 124

Red Rooster Scarf,
page 126

Rocking Robin,
page 128

Rose Corsage,
page 130

Sea Bride Bracelet,
page 134

Precious Stone
Necklace, page 136

Daisy Button Bangle,
page 138

Butterfly Friendship
Bracelet, page 140

Steampunk Butterfly
Ring, page 142

Grecian Pearls Tiara,
page 144

Pewter Heart Necklace,
page 146

Bubble Gum Charm,
page 148

Celtic Bracelet,
page 150

Calla Lily Earrings,
page 152

Statement Ring,
page 154

Beaded Felt Hairslide,
page 156

Glittery Beanie,
page 160

Christmas Stocking,
page 162

Teddy Bear, page 164

Orange Blossom,
page 168

Christmas Star,
page 170

Tate Purse, page 172

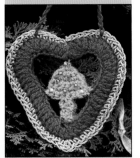
Christmas Tree Heart,
page 174

Hellebore Granny
Square Flower, page 176

Winter Beanie,
page 178

Filet Baby Blanket,
page 180

Bernie the
Christmas Elf, page 182

African Violets,
page 184

Festive Wreath,
page 186

Lottie Purse, page 188

Heart String, page 190

Anemone Granny
Square Flower, page 192

Christmas Rose,
page 198

Pretty Poodle,
page 200

Lion, page 202

Choirboy, page 204

Winter Fairy, page 206

Lovebirds, page 208

Santa Claus, page 210

Elf Boots, page 212

Owl, page 214

Red Glitter Bag, page 216

Cordelia Cat, page 218

Christmas Charms, page 222

Teddy Bear, page 224

Owl Button, page 226

Gingerbread Charms, page 228

Christmas Bear, page 230

Pizza Necklace, page 232

Melon Slice Earrings, page 234

Polar Bear, page 236

Cupcake Button, page 238

INTRODUCTION

If you love crafting of all kinds, *Quick and Easy Christmas* is the book for you. Packed full of quick and easy projects, you can make Christmas gifts for the whole family and all your friends! Choose from Stitching, Papercraft, Knitting, Jewellery making, Crochet, Sugarcraft and Polymer Clay modelling to make fabulous presents – there is such a variety that there is something to appeal to everyone.

There are useful Know-how sections at the beginning of each separate craft to give you information on materials, tools and techniques needed to make the projects.

From the Stitching projects you can make a Felt Winter Owl, a Pompom Santa or a Jelly Roll Bag; from the Papercraft projects, make a Christmas Tree Papercut, a Quilled Reindeer or a Washi Tape Card; the Knitting projects offer a Twinkling Star, some Frosty Wrist Warmers and some Penguin Boot Cuffs; the Jewellery projects include a Steampunk Butterfly, a

Pewter Heart Necklace and a Statement Ring; the Crochet projects offer a Glittery Beanie hat, a Christmas Star and a Festive Wreath; from the Sugarcraft projects you can make a Christmas Rose, a Winter Fairy and some Elf Boots; and from the Polymer Clay projects, you can make a Christmas Bear, a Cupcake Button and a Gingerbread Charm.

These are just a selection of the projects that you can make, designed by some of Search Press's most successful authors including Sue Stratford, Frances McNaughton, Val Pierce, Carolyn Schulz, Susie Johns and Alistair Macdonald.

What could be more satisfying than gifts that you have made yourself for family and friends at Christmas time!

Happy crafting!

STITCHING KNOW-HOW

Making bunting

When making pennants and bunting (see pages 20 and 36) there are some useful techniques to follow to ensure that you get good fabric shapes without too much thickness inside.

Stitching and clipping points

Sew down one side of the pennant, stopping just before you reach the stitching line for the other side. (If you find it hard to judge the position of this stitching line, measure and mark it with a fabric marker before you start sewing.) Lift the presser foot and turn the fabric so that the foot is parallel to the top edge. Turn the hand wheel on the machine to make a single stitch, which should bring you to the second stitching line. Lift the presser foot again and turn the fabric to sew the second side of the pennant.

Trim the point off the pennant just below the stitching. Cut away some fabric from the seam allowances either side of the point.

Clipping corners

Trim the corner off the flag just beyond the stitching. Cut away some fabric from the seam allowances either side of the corner.

Clipping curves

Cut small wedges out of the seam allowances, cutting up close to the stitching. Space the wedges quite close together on tighter curves and further apart on softer ones.

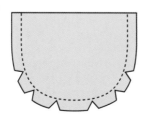

Free machine embroidery

This technique allows you to use the sewing machine like a drawing tool as you can move the fabric under the needle in any direction. In most cases, simply set the machine to a straight stitch, attach a darning foot and drop the feed dog (but do check your machine's instructions).

Practice makes perfect with this technique: working through basic shapes such as circles, squares and triangles is a great way to start and will soon build up your confidence. The charm of this style is that you'll never create two identical pieces and each design will have its own quirky character.

Unless you are a very experienced machine embroiderer, it is best to place your work in an embroidery hoop when using fabrics with body.

See page 40 for this charming Felt Duck Brooch.

Useful stitches

A number of projects in this section use some simple hand stitches, which are shown below.

Back stitch

Running stitch

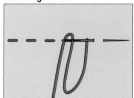

Seed stitch

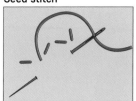

Chain stitch

Stab stitch

French knots

Oversewing

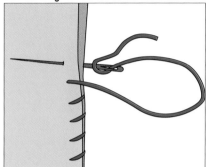

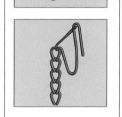

Blanket stitch

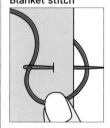

Couching stitch

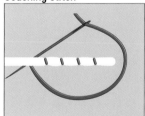

Silk ribbon embroidery

A linen-cotton mix fabric is ideal for silk ribbon embroidery. You will need an emboidery hoop, chenille needles, silk ribbon and embroidery threads to provide texture.

Other items used are a pair of small, sharp scissors, paper scissors for the templates, a fine, sharp pencil, ruler or tape measure and dressmaking pins.

Cutting and anchoring ribbon

Always cut ribbon at an angle of 45° to prevent fraying, and use a short length – 12in (30cm) is ideal. To begin, 2mm and 4mm ribbon is knotted at one end. For the wider 7mm and 13mm ribbon, a short end (tag end) is threaded into a size 18 or 13 needle and pulled sharply through to the back of the fabric, then secured with a few small stitches behind the petal about to be worked using a fabric-toned embroidery thread. The ribbon needs to sit smoothly on the right side of the fabric.

Making pompoms

You can make pompoms using either the traditional method with cardboard, or with plastic pompom makers. This shows you the traditional method, which you can use for the Pompom Cupcakes on page 22 and the Pompom Santa on page 32.

1 Cut out two identical cardboard discs to the diameter of the intended pompom. Mark out a smaller circle in the centre of each disc. This will form a hole to allow yarn to be passed through. As a rule of thumb, this circle should be half the diameter of the outer circle. Cut the inner circles out.

2 Hold the two cardboard discs together and start to wind your chosen yarn round the rings. Cover the ring entirely until the hole in the centre has almost disappeared.

3 With fabric scissors, cut through the yarn between the cardboard discs round the outer edge. Cut round the entire circumference, releasing all of the yarn and revealing the cardboard discs.

4 Tie a spare piece of yarn between the discs to secure the middle of the pompom.

5 Once knotted securely, tear the cardboard to release the pompom.

6 Finish by trimming the pompom into a neat ball.

Faux Fur

The Fur Scatter Pillow on page 42 uses faux fur, and there are some important things to know before you start working with this lovely fabric.

Cutting faux fur

Always use a scalpel to cut fur and never scissors. If you use scissors, you will end up cutting the long fibres off. Always cut on the reverse side of the fur.

As you cut with the knife, use your other hand to hold the fur above the knife. Use your fingers to gently pull the cut line apart (see right). Holding the work in this way is also important to counteract the drag or pull that a knife produces. Using a knife also reduces the amount of loose fur produced during the cutting process.

Hair direction and pile consideration

As a general rule, fur should always face or point down towards the ground. If the hair has a much shorter pile, this rule can be reversed because it will give the illusion that the colour of the fur is deeper and more intense (rather like using velvet).

As fur is similar to hair and varies in length, this needs to be considered when plotting out a pattern or template. If you wish the fur to stop at a certain depth or level, you will need to deduct the hair length from the base of a pattern. This is where the hair will naturally overhang. If you do not do this, you will end up with a much deeper trim.

Attaching the lining/bias tape

Attaching lining/bias tape not only allows you to finish the raw edges of fur, but it also helps give the fur 'body' and the feeling of fullness. The process stabilises the outer edges and means you do not need to use an iron (which should never be used on fur, whether it be real or faux). This technique is used throughout the projects found within this book.

The tape should always be sewn directly onto the fur side to avoid puckering. When attaching the tape, comb any stray fur inwards under the tape while you sew. This prevents the fur becoming trapped within the seam, which will look ugly when the tape has been 'rolled' to the reverse of the fur (see right). The back of the blades of a pair of dressmaking snips are an ideal tool to comb back the fur.

'Rolling' the fur

'Rolling' the fur is a very important technique. After the lining/bias tape has been attached, roll the tape towards the reverse side of the fur. As your thumb folds the tape over, gently roll a little of the fur edge with the tape. Tack/baste the tape to the fur backing with a running stitch ½in (1cm) away from the seam. This will achieve a plumper edge and prevent the fur from looking flat.

FLOWERY BUNTING

Materials:

For each pennant: two pieces of floral cotton fabric measuring at least 6¾ x 8in (17 x 20cm)

Sewing thread

¾in (2cm) floral bias binding the required length of the bunting, allowing for ties at each end

Tools:

Pencil

Ruler

Paper scissors

Card for template

Fabric marker

Fabric scissors

Pins

Sewing machine

Iron

Knitting needle (optional)

Instructions:

1 On the card draw a triangle 6¾in (17cm) wide across the top and 8in (20cm) from top to tip. Cut this out to make a template. Use the template and fabric marker to draw as many pennants as you need on to the fabric. Cut out each one and pin them together in pairs, right sides together, matching all edges.

2 Set the sewing machine to a medium straight stitch. Taking a ⅜in (1cm) seam allowance, machine-sew down both sloping sides of each pennant, leaving the straight top edge open.

3 Trim the seam allowances and clip the point of each pennant (see page 16). Turn each pennant right side out and press flat. You will find the end of a knitting needle useful for turning out the point, but be careful not to push the needle right through the fabric.

4 Set the sewing machine to a medium zigzag stitch. Sew across the top of each pennant to stiffen the edge and prevent it from fraying.

5 Slip the top edge of each pennant into the binding, spacing the pennants evenly. Pin each one in place. Turn under and pin the ends of the binding to neaten them.

6 Set the sewing machine to a medium straight stitch. Starting at one end of the binding, machine along it close to the open edge, sewing over each pennant and taking out the pins as you go. Press the bunting.

Make this colourful bunting in any fabric you wish. Choose contrasting and complementary designs for a burst of colour, whatever the weather outdoors.

POMPOM CUPCAKES

Materials:

1 x 100g ball each of light brown and red yarn

Scrap of yarn in a bright colour

Small amounts of white and yellow felt

Tools:

Fabric scissors

Paper and pinking shears

Tailor's chalk

1in (25mm) and 1¾in (45mm) pompom makers (optional)

Pins

Sewing needle

Glue gun

Card for templates

Instructions:

1 Photocopy the templates provided below and transfer them to a piece of card. Cut out and set aside.

2 With red yarn, make up one 1in (25mm) pompom (using the pompom maker or the cardboard method if preferred). This will form a cherry for the top of the cupcake. Using light brown yarn and a 1¾in (45mm) pompom maker, make a larger pompom. Trim and shape each one into a neat ball and set aside.

3 Lay the cupcake case template on to some yellow felt and mark out with chalk. With fabric scissors cut out the sides and base curve of the case. To create the serrated top of the case, carefully cut this top curve with pinking shears (shown by the zigzag red line on the template). Bring the short edges together, overlapping by about ⅛in

(4mm), and pin to hold. Hand sew with a running stitch to secure in place, and remove the pin.

4 Take a scrap of bright-coloured yarn and wrap it around the felt ring. Use the jagged tops as a guide. Leave two jagged points in between each line of yarn. Continue to wrap the yarn around the whole case until you reach the start. Tie both loose ends of yarn inside the case to secure. Trim the ends and rearrange evenly around the base of the case.

5 Cut out the icing shape from white felt. Sew the cherry to the middle to secure. Assemble the cupcake by gluing the brown pompom into the case, followed by the icing topper complete with cherry.

23

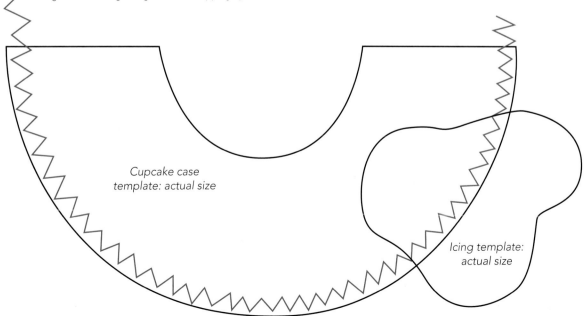

Cupcake case template: actual size

Icing template: actual size

You could fill these owls with herbs or spices such as dried lavender or cinnamon to fill your home with a festive aroma.

FELT WINTER OWL

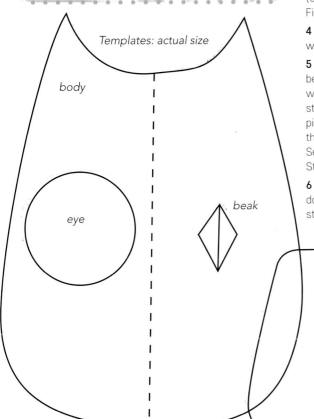

Templates: actual size

body

eye

beak

wings

Materials:

9½ x 4¼in (24 x 11cm) of brown or white felt for the body and wings

1¼ x 2¼in (3 x 6cm) of contrasting felt for the eyes

7¾ x ¾in (20 x 2cm) of red felt for the scarf

Scrap of brown or black felt for the beak and pupils

Two ¾in (2cm) diameter wooden buttons for the eyes (optional)

6–7¾in (15–20cm) of thin ribbon or string

Embroidery cotton

About ½oz (8g) of toy filling

Tools:

Paper, fabric and embroidery scissors

Embroidery needle

Instructions:

1 Copy the templates below and cut them out. Transfer the shapes to the felt and cut two body pieces and two wings from the large piece of felt, and one beak and two eyes from the smaller pieces of felt.

2 Take the long piece of red felt and, with your embroidery scissors, cut little fringes along both ends. Do not cut them too thin or they will tear and fall off. About ¼in (5–8mm) wide is ideal.

3 For button eyes, lay the felt circles on the front body piece with the wooden buttons on top. Secure them to the body with a few stitches through the buttonholes. For felt eyes, place the felt circles on the front body piece and stitch them in place with long straight stitches starting from the centre and radiating outwards. Cut a small circle of brown or black felt for each pupil, about ¼–½in (0.5–1cm) diameter, and stitch in the centre of the eye. Finish with a French knot.

4 Place the beak just below the eyes and sew it in place with a few overhand stitches.

5 Take your length of ribbon and fold it in half. This will be the hanging loop. Place it at the top of the head on the wrong side of the back body piece. Make a couple of small stitches to secure it. Do not cut your thread. Put the front piece on top of the back piece, wrong sides together, with the ends of the hanging loop sandwiched between the two. Sew all the way round with blanket or overhand stitch. Stuff the owl with toy filling before closing it completely.

6 Place the wings on the sides of the owl about halfway down and sew them along the top with a few overhand stitches.

7 Tie the scarf around the neck of the owl to keep it nice and warm.

SCOTTIE DOG BROOCH

Materials:

Dog-coloured felt

Embroidery thread

Toy stuffing

Ribbon

Button

Brooch finding

Tools:

Fabric scissors

Embroidery needle

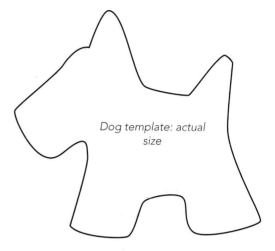

Dog template: actual size

Instructions:

1 Using the template (right), cut out two dog body shapes from the coloured felt.

2 Lay one piece on top of the other, aligning them perfectly, and secure them in the centre with a pin.

3 Starting at the top of the tail and moving anti-clockwise, hand sew a blanket stitch around the outer edge. Pause when you reach the bottom of the dog's back leg. Remove the pin.

4 Fill the shape with a little toy stuffing and continue the blanket stitch until the dog is stitched closed.

5 Cut a length of ribbon 5in (12.5cm) long and cut one end at a sharp diagonal angle. Thread the button onto the ribbon.

6 Place the ribbon around the dog's neck and secure it at the back with a double knot. Cut off any excess ribbon, snipping the ends at an angle to prevent them from fraying.

7 Attach the brooch finding.

Tip: filling your dog

Use a knitting needle or pencil to insert the toy stuffing; use only very small amounts at a time and you will fill the shape more evenly.

Try using different colours and button shapes to change the look and personalise the brooch. Or try adding a bell to create a lovely festive brooch for Christmas time!

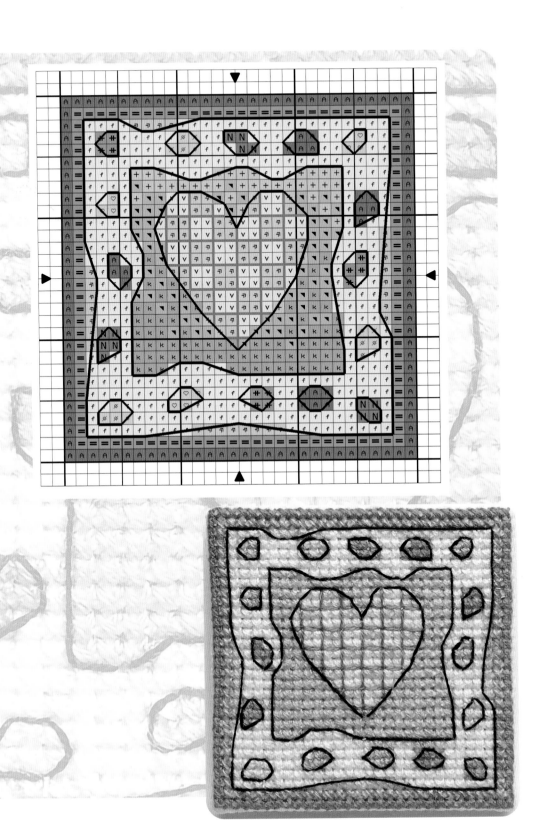

CROSS STITCH HEART

Materials:

- 14 count Aida fabric (evenweave and canvas can be used as alternatives)
- Anchor embroidery thread (see colours required, right); there are conversion charts readily available for different brands of thread such as DMC or Madeira, if preferred

Tools:

Size 24 or 26 tapestry needle

Stitching notes:

Stitch count: 30 x 30.

Design area: 2⅛ x 2⅛in (5.4 x 5.4cm) at 55sts per 4in (10cm).

Where two colours are shown against a symbol, use one strand of each colour. One symbol on a square represents one full cross stitch worked in the colour specified. One full stitch on Aida is worked over one square, while on evenweave it is worked over two threads.

Colour key:

♡	Navy Blue vy lt (129)
Y	Burnt Orange lt + Burnt Orange ultra vy lt (301 + 386)
ㄱ	Tangerine vy lt (311)
f	Burnt Orange ultra vy lt (386)
k	Gold vy lt (874)
+	Old Gold lt (891)
◣	Gold vy lt + Old Gold lt (874 + 891)
A	Terracotta lt (338)
∅	Pink lt (49)
N	Laurel Green med (261)
＃	Lavender lt (108)
=	Tangerine vy lt + Terracotta lt (311 + 338)

Instructions:

1 Find the centre of your fabric by folding it in half lengthways and widthways, and mark the centre with a pin. The centre of the design can be found on the chart by following the arrows on each side, top and bottom. Mark the centre of the chart and begin stitching at the centre of the design.

2 When you have completed the cross stitch design, you can start on the outlines. All of the outlines are in long stitch with one strand of Black (403). The exception is the grid within the heart, which is stitched in one strand of Terracotta lt (338). Stitch this before any of the black outlines.

3 When you have finished stitching your design, wash it gently in warm water and washing-up liquid, trying not to crease the fabric. Rinse the piece thoroughly and roll the fabric in a towel to soak up the excess water. Place it face down on a towel and press with a hot iron, being careful not to distort the fabric.

How to work cross stitch

All cross stitch is worked in two strands unless indicated on the key. Each cross is made up of two stitches that together form an 'X'. The bottom stitch is worked from lower left to upper right, and the top stitch is worked from upper left to lower right.

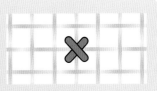

Cross stitch

JELLY ROLL BAG

Materials:

Nine 2½in (6.5cm) squares of light-coloured fabric

Nine 2½in (6.5cm) squares of dark-coloured fabric

1 Jelly Roll strip for the gusset, 2½ x 22in
(6.5 x 56cm)

Lining fabric, 13 x 7¼in (33 x 18.5cm)

Fabric for loop, 2½ x 3in (6.5 x 7.5cm) cut in half lengthways
to make a strip 1¼in (3.25cm) wide

Fabric for handles, 2½ x 22in (6.5 x 56cm)

Button for closure, 1in (2.5cm) diameter

Tools:

Basic sewing kit: sewing needles, pins, a ruler or
tape measure, a small pair of scissors, fabric
scissors, sewing thread

Sewing machine

Rotary cutting mat, ruler and cutter (optional)

Pen to mark fabric

Iron and ironing mat

Size:

7 x 7in (18 x 18cm) excluding handles

Instructions:

1 On the back of the light squares, draw a diagonal line from corner to corner. Place these on top of the dark squares, right sides facing. Stitch along either side of the line, ¼in (0.5cm) away from the line.

2 Cut the squares in half along the drawn line and press the seams open. You will have 18 of these in total.

3 Lay nine of the squares out in three rows of three, with all the seams running in the same direction. Sew the squares together in rows, pressing the seams in alternating directions on each row. Sew the rows together to make a block. Press the seams open. Make two of these blocks, one for each side of the bag.

4 Stitch the gusset around three sides of one of the blocks, right sides facing. Press the seams towards the gusset. Repeat, sewing the other block to the gusset. Press the seams towards the gusset.

5 To make the loop for the button fastening, fold the fabric in half lengthways, wrong sides together, and fold the raw edges into the fold. Press and machine stitch along the edge.

6 Fold the strip in half to form a loop and pin it centrally on the back of the bag on the wrong side, just below the top edge. The loop should be pointing downwards into the bag.

7 Now make two handles. Fold the piece of fabric for the handles in half lengthways, wrong sides together, and fold the edges into the middle as you did for the loop. Press and machine stitch along each edge to secure.

8 Cut the fabric in half widthways to make two handles. Pin these on the top edge of the bag, one on each side. Align the raw edges and position them in the middle of the two outside squares. The handles will be facing down into the bag.

9 To make the lining, fold the lining fabric right sides together so that it measures 6½ x 7¼in (16.5 x 18.5cm) and machine up each side. On one side leave a 2in (5cm) gap in the middle for turning through later.

10 To shape the lining base, refold the lining so that the seams are in the middle and mark 1in (2.5cm) on either side of one of the seams across the point. Stitch across between these two marks. Secure the stitching and cut off the point leaving ¼in (0.5cm) seam allowance. Repeat for the second seam.

11 Place the outer bag inside the lining, right sides together. Match the side seams and pin. Sew around the top of the bag.

12 Turn the bag right-side out, sew the opening in the lining closed and press.

13 Sew the button on the bag about ½in (1cm) down from the top edge.

POMPOM SANTA

Materials:

- 1 x 100g ball each of red and white yarn
- Small amounts of red and beige bulky (chunky) yarn
- Five 11¾in (30cm) chenille sticks
- One wooden ball, 2in (5cm) in diameter
- 7¾in (20cm) length of gold craft wire
- Small toilet roll inner
- 3⅜in (85mm) and 1in (25mm) pompom makers (optional)
- Long, large-eyed sewing needle
- Black marker pen
- Pink blending pencil
- Wire cutters

Tools:

- Paper scissors
- Glue gun

Instructions:

1 Start by making a frame for the hat. Lay three chenille sticks across each other to form a star shape. Twist the sticks together and mould into a cone shape. Cut a ⅜in (1cm) section from the toilet roll inner (keep it as a ring) and attach the chenille stick ends, spacing them evenly round the circumference of the cardboard, by folding them under and round the card. Once secure, bend the cone shape over to make the base for the hat. Cover the entire shape with the chunky red yarn, concealing the card and sticks. Secure the yarn by gluing.

2 To make the rim of the hat, cover two chenille sticks in white yarn. Fold about 3in (7.5cm) of each end of the sticks into the centre so that they meet in the middle and flatten the sticks using your fingers. Then hold both sticks together lengthways and wind more white yarn around to encase them. Continue until you reach a desired thickness. Bend this piece round the base of the red hat and secure by stitching at the rear with spare white yarn.

3 Using the 3⅜in (85mm) pompom maker, make one pompom in red yarn. Using the 1in (25mm) maker, complete a second pompom in white yarn. Trim into neat balls using fabric scissors. Glue the wooden ball on to the top of the red pompom. Draw on the eyes and add some rosy cheeks using the pen and pencil. Glue the white pompom to the end of the hat.

4 The same method is used to construct both the beard and hair. Cut ten lengths of beige chunky yarn approximately 7¾in (20cm) long. Tie the yarn in the centre to combine and secure. Make a second bunch of yarn in the same way. Glue one bunch onto Santa's face to create a beard. The knot should face towards the wood to conceal it. Spread the yarn across the face, sticking it into position with some glue. Trim the beard into shape, using the photograph for guidance. Glue the second bunch to Santa's head, using the same method, to create the hair. Glue the hat onto the head and trim Santa's hair as desired. Sew a loop of red yarn on to the hat to allow it to hang.

5 The final touch is to construct a pair of spectacles. Take the craft wire and wrap it round a pen twice, about 2in (5cm) away from one of the ends. This will create one of the lenses. Leave a small gap and repeat the process to form the spectacles. Cut the wire 1in (2.5cm) away from each lens and bend inwards. Place the spectacles on to Santa's head and glue into position.

This festive red alternative flower requires only the very simplest of embroidery stitches to create a charmingly naïve effect. You can stitch any pattern of running stitches you like on to the felt, though it works best if the stitching relates to the shape of the flower.

DAISY BROOCH

Materials:

Two pieces of purple felt measuring at least 4in (10cm) square

Stranded pink and blue embroidery thread

Craft glue

Brooch finding

Tools:

Paper scissors

Fabric scissors

Embroidery needle

Small, stiff-bristle paintbrush

Instructions:

1 Copy the daisy motif and cut it out to make a template. Lay the template on a piece of purple felt and draw and cut out one flower.

2 Split lengths of embroidery thread into groups of three strands. Using one group at a time, embroider the cut-out flower as shown with a simple design in running stitch. Repeat in a second colour.

3 Sew the finding to the centre of the remaining piece of felt. Lay this piece on the back of the cut-out flower with the finding in the required position and make sure that all of the cut-out flower is covered by the finding piece of felt.

4 Using the paintbrush, paint craft glue all over the back of the cut-out flower, brushing it right up to the edges of the petals. You will need to work quite quickly before the glue dries. Press the glued flower on to the other piece of felt, ensuring the finding is in the right place. Leave to dry.

5 Cut out the backing felt, carefully cutting around the flower.

Daisy motif: actual size

Materials:

Red and green floral fabric, 4 x 4¾in (10 x 12cm) per flag, and the same to use as a lining

Red bias binding ¾in (2cm) wide, measure to the desired length of bunting, plus ties at the ends

Large red jacket buttons

Green embroidery thread

Sewing thread to match the bias binding

Tools:

Pencil

Ruler

Card for template

Fabric marker

Pins

Paper and fabric scissors

Iron

Sewing machine

Large upholstery needle or knitting needle

Hand sewing needle

CHRISTMAS BUNTING

Instructions:

1 Start by transferring the triangle template (right) on to card and cut it out.

2 With the fabric pinned right sides together, place the template on top and carefully draw around all of the edges using a fabric marker. Remove the template and secure the two layers together with pins, then cut round the marked lines. Repeat this process until you have enough flags for your bunting length.

3 Set a sewing machine to a medium-sized stitch. Take a flag and start to sew down one of the sides. Seam allowance has been added to the template at ⅜in (1cm). As you reach the end of the first side, stop the stitching ⅜in (1cm) away from the base of the work. Lift the foot and turn the flag towards you and continue stitching down the opposite edge. Now clip the excess fabric from the tip of the flag and turn right side out. Use the eye of a large upholstery or knitting needle to ease the tip of the flag out. Take care not to push too hard as this may result in the needle coming through the work. Press the flag flat and trim away the protruding seam allowance to maintain a straight edge along the top. Repeat this process until all of the flags have been completed.

4 Using an iron, carefully press the bias binding in half lengthwise, matching the edges together. Sandwich each flag between the folded bias and pin into position. Space evenly and alternate red flags with green flags; I have spaced mine 1in (2.5cm) apart. Make sure you leave enough free bias at the start and finish to allow for ties. Sew the bias binding together along the entire length using a sewing machine set to a medium straight stitch. Stitch as close to the edge as you can. Press the bunting flat.

5 Between each flag, hand sew a red jacket button in the centre of the bias binding using green embroidery thread.

Triangle template: actual size

Pink and white are traditional colours for sugar mice, but you could also make a grey mouse that is closer to the real thing!

FELTIE MOUSE

Materials:

Fleece

Merino in black and pink

Pale pink felt fabric

2 black seed beads

Black and pink thread

Tools:

Felting needle

Foam block

Scissors

Sewing needle

Beading needle

Instructions:

1 First you need to form a low, flat-bottomed egg shape with fleece, tapering it at the end for the nose. Take a small handful of fleece. Pull out the wool fibres into a long strand, then curl it tightly into a bundle. Place the item on a working surface such as a needle felting base, an old cushion or foam block. Needle the wool repeatedly with your felting needle, inserting the needle in and out with a straight up and down movement. Move the piece around to work at it from all sides. Add more wool in stages, layering and needling in thin strands to achieve the desired size and shape. It should start to form a coarse-looking, fairly firmly packed shape. Check your sizing and also if the shape is firm enough. Keep comparing with the photograph (below) and amend as you go.

2 Cover the shape with pink merino wool.

3 Cut teardrop-shaped ears and a 3½in (9cm) long strip for a tail from the pink felt fabric.

4 Take the felt ears and check where they will be positioned at the front of the mouse. Take the felting needle and secure each ear in place by needling repeatedly at the point of the teardrop shape. This will make a small indent and will also slightly cup the ear. Take the tail and sew it firmly into place at the back of the mouse body using the sewing needle and pink thread.

5 For the whiskers, thread the sewing needle with black thread. Do not knot the end. Sew into one side of the nose leaving a ¾in (2cm) strand at the entry site. Pull through to the opposite side through the nose, double back through to the original entry site and then back out of the second hole. Cut the thread, leaving a ¾in (2cm) strand. Repeat three times.

6 Needle felt some black wool for the nose.

7 Use a beading needle to sew on black seed beads for the eyes.

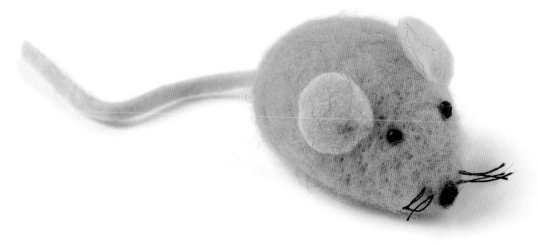

FELT DUCK BROOCH

Materials:

Tracing paper

White or cream felt,
   3¼ x 3¼in (8 x 8cm)

Scraps of orange felt

Calico, 7 x 7in (18 x 18cm)

Wadding/batting, 3¼ x 3¼in
   (8 x 8cm)

Backing felt, 7 x 7in (18 x 18cm)

Black thread

Brooch back

Tools:

Embroidery hoop 6¼in (16cm) in
   diameter

Sewing machine

Paper scissors

Fabric scissors

Embroidery scissors

Pins

Needle

Tacking/basting thread

41

Instructions:

1 Trace the duck template and cut it out from the white or cream felt, leaving a ½in (1cm) border.

2 Stretch the calico on the hoop. Lay the wadding/batting centrally on top of the calico.

3 Lay the felt duck shape on top of the wadding/batting and the paper pattern on top of the felt. Pin through all layers.

4 Cut the orange scraps slightly bigger than the beak and feet shapes. Lay these pieces in place under the pattern, tacking/basting in place.

5 Sew the outline. Starting by the top of the beak, follow the outline around the head, sew down the curving line into the body and retrace to join the outline. Continue around the tail feathers and down to the right leg. Travel up to the top of the right leg, back down the leg and around to the lower point of the foot. Stitch up into the foot and back down. Continue around the foot up into the leg and back down to re-join the outline. Continue the outline sewing the left leg in a similar way, around the front and up to the neck. Continue around the beak, travelling across and back when you reach the top where it joins the body, finishing at the starting point.

6 Carefully tear away the tracing paper pattern.

7 To make the eye, sew several stitches in a circular movement.

8 Carefully cut around the duck outline, leaving a small margin.

9 Trim away the excess wadding/batting and calico so that they sit just under the felt.

10 Place the work on the backing felt stretched in a hoop. Pin and stitch the outline. Start at the top of the beak and follow all the way around and back to the starting point.

11 Trim away any excess felt.

12 Sew a brooch back onto the centre of the backing felt.

Duck template:
actual size

FUR SCATTER PILLOW

Materials:

Faux chocolate chinchilla fur

39½in (1m) of backing fabric

Four checked tweeds, each 4¼ x 4¼in
(11 x 11cm)

Toy stuffing or a made-to-measure pillow pad

Tools:

Fabric scissors

Scalpel

Sewing thread

Sewing machine

Chalk

Long, strong pins

Ruler, tape measure and set square

Iron

Size:

Finished pillow measures 15 x 15in
(38 x 38cm)

Instructions:

1 Sew the four squares of tweed together using a ½in (1cm) seam allowance. Press the seams flat at the rear with a hot iron and place to one side. Lay out the backing fabric and cut out two squares measuring 15¾ x 15¾in (40 x 40cm). Fold over 6in (15cm) along one side of the first square and press. Repeat this process for the other square and put to one side.

2 Read the instructions on working with faux fur (see page 19) before you start cutting out. Chalk out strips directly onto the fabric side of the fur with a depth of 3½in (9cm) and 15in (38cm) in length horizontally. With a set square, mitre the corners. The shorter line should measure 7¾in (20cm) in length and the longer 15in (38cm). Now add a ½in (1cm) seam allowance round all edges. You need four strips in total. The fur direction should run away from the shorter horizontal line. Cut out using a scalpel.

3 Line up the short edges of the fur strips along the four edges of the tweed. Pin and machine sew into position with a large stitch, combing any stray fur inwards as you sew. Complete all four edges. Pin the mitred corners and stitch them closed in the same manner.

4 Place the fur-trimmed tweed facing up and layer over the backing pieces. The first piece should be laid with the pressed edge facing you and resting over the middle of the pillow. Match up the outer corners and pin. Add the second backing section likewise. Machine stitch the entire pillow round the perimeter using a ½in (1cm) seam allowance, combing the fur as you stitch. Pull the work through and fill the pillow with toy stuffing or a pillow pad.

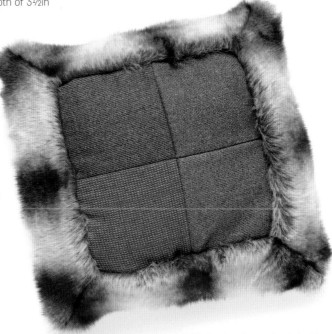

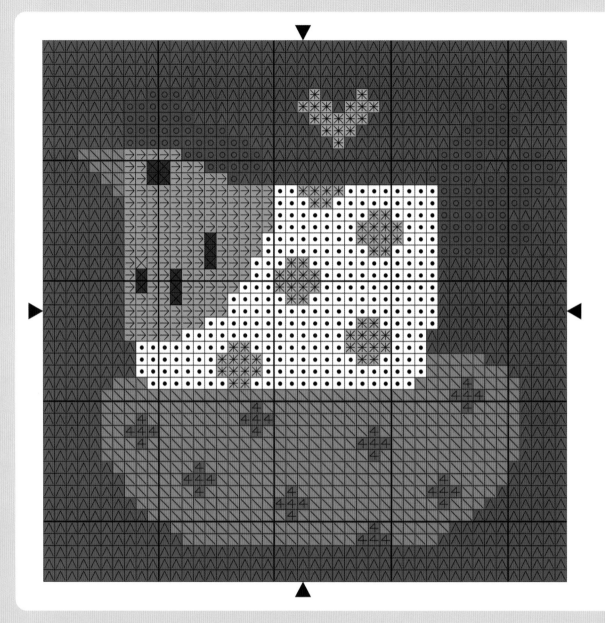

How to work half-cross tent stitch

As the name implies, this method involves creating a slanted stitch (half a cross stitch) worked diagonally. It does not matter in which direction the stitches slant as long as they all slant in the same direction. Work in rows alternately from left to right and then right to left, counting the squares and following the colour key. Each square on the graph is one slanted stitch (see above).

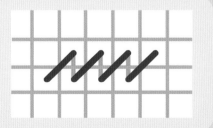

NEEDLEPOINT HEN

Materials:

10 hole per inch (2.5cm) white interlock canvas

Anchor tapestry wool (see colour key below)

Tools:

Size 18 tapestry needle

Instructions:

1 Start your stitching from the centre outwards to ensure that you fit the whole design on your measured piece of canvas. Locate the centre stitch of your graph by following the arrows on each side, top and bottom. Mark this centre stitch and start your piece from here.

2 When starting a new colour, leave a 1in (2.5cm) length of thread at the back of your work and then, while working your first row of stitches, catch this thread into the back of them to secure it in place. When ending a colour, run a 1in (2.5cm) length of wool through the stitches at the back of your work to secure and snip off.

Stitching Notes:

Stitch count: 45 x 45.

Design area: 4½ x 4½in (11.4 x 11.4 cm) at 10 sts per 1in (2.5 cm).

Each single square on the chart (opposite) represents one half-cross tent stitch. The symbol in that square represents the colour to be used, which is specified in the colour key below.

Colour key:

 White (8000)

 Light grey (8622)

 Orange (8136)

 Bright orange (8140)

 Red (8440)

 Bright blue (8804)

 Lavender (8606)

 Navy (8738)

SILK RIBBON POINSETTIA

Materials:

Small amount of black fabric (or colour of your choice)

60in (1.5m) of 13mm ribbon in red

Embroidery thread in yellow, gold and base fabric colour (black)

Needles:

Two size 13 needles,

One size 18 needle,

One size 24 needle and

One size 8 embroidery needle

Instructions:

1 Read the basic guidance for working with silk ribbon on page 17 before you start. Then, transfer the design to your fabric base. If you are using black fabric, use a white pencil to transfer the design. Pin the template on to the fabric and mark the position of the petals. If you are using black fabric, it is helpful if a red thread is used to work a ring of small stitches to mark the centre circle on the fabric.

2 Cut a 12in (30cm) length of red ribbon at an angle, thread a short end into a size 13 needle and take it through to the back of the fabric at X of petal 1. Secure the ribbon end with a few small stitches behind the petal about to be worked. Now lay the ribbon in position and take the needle down through the centre of the ribbon at Y, place the eye end of a second large needle in the loop and continue pulling the ribbon round the needle. Stop pulling when all the ribbon is pulled through, remove the needle and very gently pull the ribbon to form a tip to the petal, then stop pulling the ribbon again. Now secure the ribbon with a few small stitches behind the petal just worked and cut the ribbon at an angle.

3 Continue to work alternate petals 2, 3, 4, 5, 6 and 7, fastening off after each one. Now work petal A as before, but a little shorter and very slightly raised, remembering to finish off after each petal is worked. Work the remaining petals, B to G, in order.

4 To make the flower centre, thread six strands of yellow embroidery thread into a size 18 needle and knot one end. Work 2-loop French knots to fill the centre. Using gold thread, add a few 2-loop French knots at random to complete, then fasten off.

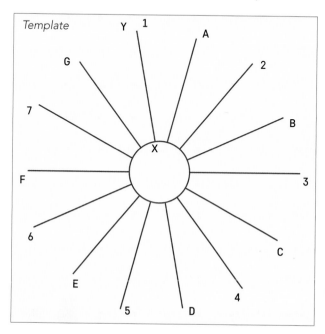

Template

CHRISTMAS TEA LIGHT

Materials:

Small amount of white yarn

Three sheets of burgundy felt,
   8¼ x 11¾in (210 x 297mm)

Felt scraps in two shades
   of green

6 large gold sleigh bells

2¼yd (2m) of red satin ribbon
   ⅛in (3mm) wide

One small glass with a 9in (23cm)
   circumference at the base

Battery-operated tea light (optional)

Tools:

One sheet of paper, 8¼ x 11¾in
   (210 x 297mm)

Fabric and paper scissors

Tailor's chalk

1in (25mm) pompom maker

Hand sewing needles

Glue gun

Ruler

Pair of compasses

*Mistletoe template:
actual size*

Instructions:

1 Photocopy the mistletoe template (right) and set aside. Now make your own template for the base of the tea light holder. Set the compasses to 2¾in (7cm) wide and draw a circle on to paper. Use the circle to mark out three base sections on to burgundy felt. Neatly cut out all three and layer together, securing with a glue gun. On a separate sheet of felt, mark out a rectangle measuring 4¾ x 9in (12 x 23cm). Cut out and fold together lengthways, gluing to secure, and allow to dry.

2 With some chalk, mark a central line down the folded felt along the longest edge. Using fabric scissors, cut straight lines at ½in (1cm) intervals from the raw edge in towards the chalked line. Bring the short edges together and secure by sewing, but only down to the chalk line. This should form a cuff to grip the base of the glass. The raw edges should fan away from the glass. Place the cuffed glass centrally onto the base section and glue the fanned rays to secure into place. Remove the glass so that you can decorate the holder.

3 Make up six 1in (25mm) pompoms in white yarn, trimmed into neat balls. Mark out as many mistletoe leaves in green felt as you require (I have used six per shade of green) and cut them out. Cut the ribbon into 11¾in (30cm) lengths and bunch together, securing at the base with a stitch.

4 Now all of your components are ready – pompoms, mistletoe leaves, sleigh bells and ribbon bunches – simply arrange and sew them on to the base. Try a few options first by pinning them down before you decide on a final composition. Please note that if you have a slightly wider bottomed glass, all you have to do is increase the length of the cuff and possibly enlarge the base section a little. Never use a real tea light without the glass.

This set looks stylish with a very simple embroidered design. If you are feeling more confident with your embroidery, try stitching a more intricate design or create a unique family monogram.

FELT PLACE SETTING

Materials:

- 9¾ x 6in (25 x 15cm) of grey felt
- 4 x 4in (10 x 10cm) of white felt
- 23½in (60cm) of red ric-rac
- Red embroidery cotton
- Fabric glue

Tools:

- Paper, fabric and embroidery scissors
- Zigzag scissors
- Dressmaking pins
- Embroidery needle
- Pencil, ruler and pair of compasses
- Paper

Instructions:

1 On your piece of paper draw a 4 x 6in (10 x 15cm) rectangle, a 6 x 2in (15 x 5cm) rectangle and two circles of 2¼in (6cm) and 1¼in (3cm) in diameter. Cut out these templates and transfer them to the felt. Cut two large rectangles and one small rectangle from the grey felt using fabric scissors, and one circle of each size from the white felt using the zigzag scissors.

2 For the cutlery pouch, place the large circle on one of the large rectangles, roughly in the middle. Starting from the centre of the circle and going through both layers, make a cross (+) using long straight stitches and then an x shape. This will make a lovely star. Add a French knot at the end of each stitch, leaving a small gap.

3 Place a thin line of fabric glue about ¾in (1.5cm) from the top edge, and another one ¾in (1.5cm) from the bottom edge of the felt rectangle.

Stick on the ric-rac by pressing it down firmly for a few seconds. Leave about ½in (1cm) of ric-rac sticking out at the sides.

4 Place this grey rectangle on top of the other one, wrong sides together, and sew them together on three sides with a blanket stitch. Leave the top open. Tuck the ends of the ric-rac inside as you stitch for a clean finish.

5 For the napkin ring, place the small circle in the middle of the small rectangle of felt and repeat step 2 for the stitching.

6 Repeat step 3 to attach the ric-rac close to the long edges.

7 Close the napkin ring at the back by overlapping it slightly and sewing together with a few cross stitches.

Create a vintage look using a piece of old lace, soft colours and lovely French knots as the decorative outer stitch (see brown brooch). These pretty little badges also make wonderful wedding favours at a vintage-themed wedding celebration.

HEART BROOCH

Heart motif template: actual size

Instructions:

1 Secure the neutral-coloured lightweight fabric in the embroidery hoop.

2 Cut a circle of coloured lightweight fabric: use either the manufacturer's guide for size if using a badge machine, or the instructions provided if using a metal cover button. Place the circle of fabric onto the centre of the embroidery hoop.

3 Using the template above, cut out a heart shape from a piece of felt and place in the centre of the circle of fabric.

4 Using a contrasting thread colour, hand sew back stitch around the inside edge of the heart, pushing the needle through all three layers of fabric.

5 Using running stitch, carefully sew a dashed circle around the heart shape – the circle should have a diameter of about 1¼in (3cm), as it will sit right on the edge of the badge.

6 With your stitching complete, take the fabric out of the embroidery hoop and cut around the coloured circle of fabric.

7 If you are using a badge machine, follow the manufacturer's instructions to construct the badge. If you are using a metal cover button, remove the button shank with a pair of pliers and discard. Carefully fold the fabric around the button, following the instructions. Once in place, secure the cover button back and glue a brooch back to the rear using a glue gun.

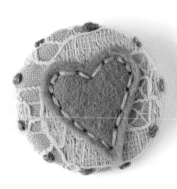

JELLY ROLL PILLOW

Materials:

Pillow fabric, linen or linen–cotton blend,
    12½ x 36½in (32 x 93cm)

Jelly Roll scraps to cover buttons, 6 pieces
    2½ x 1½in (6.5 x 4cm)

6 plastic self-cover buttons, 1¼in (3cm) in diameter

Sewing thread to match pillow fabric

13¾in (35cm) square pillow pad

Tools:

Basic sewing kit: sewing needles, pins, a ruler or tape
    measure, a small pair of scissors, fabric scissors,
    sewing thread

Sewing machine

Rotary cutting mat, ruler and cutter (optional)

Pen to mark fabric

Iron and ironing mat

Size:

12 x 12in (30.5 x 30.5cm)

Instructions:

1 On the wrong side of the fabric, turn a 4in (10cm) double hem (turn over 2in/5cm and then 2in/5cm again) on one of the short ends. Machine stitch to secure.

2 On the other short end, turn a 5in (13cm) double hem to the wrong side (turn over 2½in/6.5cm, then 2½in/6.5cm again). Machine stitch to secure, then stitch along the folded edge, ⅛in (0.25cm) in.

3 On the deepest hem end of the fabric on the right side, mark and stitch six buttonholes. These should be approximately 1½in (4cm) apart. To space them evenly, measure from the middle out towards the raw edges.

4 Lay the fabric wrong-side up and fold in the edge with the buttonholes by 5in (13cm). Fold in the other end by 10in (25.5cm). The buttonholed end should overlap the longer end. Pin in place and then stitch along the raw edge to secure. You can zigzag to neaten if you like.

5 Turn the pillow cover right side out and press.

6 Make the buttons by covering them in the Jelly Roll scraps following the button manufacturer's instructions.

7 Mark the button positions through the buttonholes, and stitch the buttons in place.

8 Insert the pillow pad and do the buttons up.

These pretty pegs are quick and easy to make – if the postman brings more cards than you anticipated, just make a few more!

POMPOM CARD PEGS

Materials:

Small amounts of of red and white yarn

Red double-sided satin ribbon, ½in (1.5cm) wide, the desired length

Scraps of light and dark green felt

Six wooden spring-loaded laundry pegs

Tools:

Paper scissors

1in (25mm) pompom maker

Glue gun

Pencil and tailor's chalk

Craft paper or card

Instructions:

1 Start by deciding how long you wish the ribbon that will suspend and display your Christmas cards to be. Tie a knotted loop at either end to allow it to hang and place it to one side.

2 Decide on a number of pegs to make. For each peg, use either red or white yarn to determine the berry type.

3 Either trace or photocopy the holly leaf template below onto some craft paper or card, then cut it out using paper scissors. Use this template and tailor's chalk to mark out as many leaves on the scraps of felt as you require. As a ratio, I have used three leaves per peg and 2:1 per colour. Cut out all the leaves and place to one side.

4 To complete a berry, make a pompom using either red or white yarn and a 1in (25mm) pompom maker. Make two berries per peg. Trim the pompoms into neat balls and set aside.

5 Assemble each peg by layering three leaves, alternating the colours. Attach the leaves to the peg using the glue gun. At the same time, glue two berries together and then on to the holly leaves. See the photographs for guidance on positioning leaves and berries.

6 Complete this process until you have enough pegs, then hang your cards to dazzle your guests!

Holly leaf template: actual size

Gingham fabric is great if you are not a confident embroiderer, as the square pattern gives you a grid to work the stitches on. If embroidery isn't your thing, make a simpler version of this flower, like the turquoise one here, using a motif from a printed fabric to decorate the button. This bright, fresh-looking flower makes a great decoration for any bag.

FABRIC BUTTON FLOWER

Materials:

Piece of medium-weight pink cotton gingham fabric with small checks, 6in (15cm) square

1½in (38mm) self-cover button

Embroidery threads

Craft glue

Lightweight pink cotton gingham fabric with large checks, 22 x 4in (55 x 10cm)

Length of green ric-rac to fit button circumference

Sewing threads to match fabrics and ric-rac

Brooch finding

Tools:

Pair of compasses

Embroidery hoop 4in (10cm) in diameter

Embroidery needle

Fabric scissors

Hand-sewing needle

Sewing machine

Instructions:

1 Using the compasses, draw a central 2¾in (7cm) diameter circle on the medium-weight gingham fabric. Put the fabric into the hoop. Use simple embroidery stitches to sew a design into the centre of the circle. Here, I have used three strands of thread in two shades of green to work a lazy daisy surrounded by French knots and cross stitches.

2 Following the manufacturer's instructions, cover the button with the embroidered fabric, making sure you position the stitched design centrally.

3 Using tiny running stitches in thread to match the ric-rac, sew the ric-rac around the edge of the button. Tuck the ends to the back and hold them in place with craft glue.

4 Machine sew the two short ends of the long strip of fabric together to make a tube. Press the seam flat. Wrong sides facing, fold the tube in half. Run a line of running stitch along the free edges of the tube, stitching through both layers of fabric. Pull up the stitches as tightly as possible to gather the fabric and secure the thread with a few back stitches.

5 Position the button centrally on the ruffle and arrange the gathers so that they fan out evenly around the button. Thread a hand-sewing needle with thread to match the button fabric, then double and knot the thread. Starting from the back of the ruffle, bring the needle through in line with the edge of the button. Take a small stitch through the fabric at the edge of the button, under the ric-rac, and then go back down through the ruffle. Work around the button in this way, sewing it firmly to the ruffle.

6 Add a brooch finding to the back of the flower.

NEEDLEPOINT SNOWMAN

Materials:

10 hole per inch (2.5cm) white interlock canvas

Anchor tapestry wool (see colour key below)

Tools:

Size 18 tapestry needle

Colour key:

	White (8000)		Pale blue (8802)
	Sugar pink (8484)	4	Bright blue (8804)
V	Red (8440)		Denim blue (8644)
✳	Bright orange (8140)	O	Purple (8588)
X	Sage green (9094)	■	Black (9796)

Instructions:

1 Start your stitching from the centre outwards to ensure that you fit the whole design on your measured piece of canvas. Locate the centre stitch of your graph by following the arrows on each side, top and bottom. Mark this centre stitch and start your piece from here.

2 When starting a new colour, leave a 1in (2.5cm) length of thread at the back of your work and then, while working your first row of stitches, catch this thread into the back of them to secure it in place. When ending a colour, run a 1in (2.5cm) length of wool through the stitches at the back of your work to secure and snip off.

Stitching Notes:

Stitch count: 44 x 52.

Design area: 4⁷⁄₁₆ x 5¼ in (11.2 x 13.2 cm) at 10 sts per 1in (2.5cm).

Each single square on the chart (opposite) represents one half-cross tent stitch. The symbol in that square represents the colour to be used, which is specified in the colour key above.

See page 44 for instructions on working half-cross tent stitch.

PAPERCRAFT KNOW-HOW

There are a number of general tools and equipment that are useful for most paper crafts. These include:

A **rubber self-healing cutting mat** prevents your work or scalpel from slipping, and protects your worktop.
Tracing paper is useful for transferring images to paper or card.
A sharp **pencil** is essential for copying templates and for tracing.
Use a **metal ruler** to cut straight edges, and for accurate measuring.
A **glue stick** is used to stick designs to backing paper; **PVA glue** in a bottle with a fine-tipped applicator is used for sticking quilling paper together. Use sparingly.
A pair of **small, sharp scissors** is useful for cutting paper and card.
3D foam pads are used to raise decorations away from surface card.

Tools and materials useful for specific crafts include:

For Papercutting:

A **scalpel**, made up of a blade and handle, is the best implement to use for papercutting. **These are surgical grade blades, so please ensure you are over 18 and have read the usage instructions before starting.** Keep a good supply of disposable blades, as they quickly become blunt and must be changed regularly. For many people, a round barrel handle is more comfortable to use than a flat handle. Dispose of used blades safely using a **blade remover unit** – a plastic box that removes and stores blades without you having to touch them.

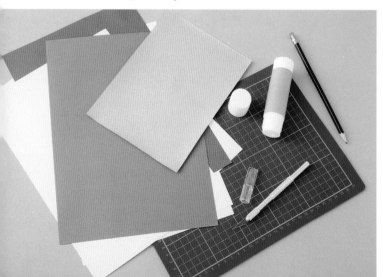

150gsm art paper is a good thickness for papercutting use. Coloured paper is great for decorative infills.

For Gift boxes and Washi tape cards:

A **Cricut machine** is great if you are making lots of gift boxes, or you can buy a **template**.
Circle punches, flower punches and **die cutters** are also useful, or you can draw and cut out your own shapes as decorations.
You may also find an **embossing stylus set** useful for decorating boxes and cards.
Ribbon, gemstones and **chalks** are also good for adding embellishments.
A **paper trimmer** makes it easy to get perfectly straight lines and evenly cut pieces.
A **bone folder and ruler** or **scoring blade** for a paper trimmer give crisply scored lines so you can easily fold your paper.
Stamps work beautifully with washi tape and allow you to customise your projects (see photograph opposite).
Washi tape is a decorative sticky tape which comes in many different colours and patterns. It can be semi-translucent and is easy to apply and remove without leaving any adhesive residue.
Baker's twine and **stickers** are also useful decorations for washi tape cards and gift boxes.

For Decoupage:

Specialist decoupage papers come in lots of different designs and colours, but you can use almost any kind of paper. **Paper napkins** are very popular, and you can also use old **book pages**, sheets of **newspaper** or **magazines**, **sheet music**, **gift-wrapping paper** or simple **tissue paper**.
Decoupage glue is glue and varnish in one product, so you can glue and seal your project at the same time. You could also use diluted **PVA glue** but if you do, you may wish to varnish your project separately.

For Quilling:

A **quilling tool** has a wooden, metal or plastic handle and a metal end with a slot in it, through which you thread the quilling paper or strips.

Cocktail sticks are useful for neatening pegs (see below) and for picking up finished coils.

Tweezers can be helpful for positioning small coils.

Use a **fine black pen** to draw facial details on designs.

Quilling papers are more usually referred to as 'quilling strips', the most popular width being ⅛in (3mm).

Chalk pastels are useful for shading card backgrounds to enhance designs.

The techniques below are very useful for quilling projects and easy to master:

Fringed flowers

This technique is used to make the Reindeer's head on page 68. Cut a series of slits along a ¼in (5mm) wide quilling strip as shown in the photograph (below). Cut two strips of paper at a time, by holding them exactly one on top of the other. Glue the top strip ¹/₁₆in (2mm) in from the strip underneath to make it easier to insert into the quilling tool. Roll up the strips. If the ends are uneven when you reach the end, trim one back to make it easier to glue down. Coat the base with glue and allow it to dry. Peel back the fringing to reveal the flower.

Eccentric circles

This technique is useful for organising the loops within a coil, and enables a coil to be shaped without losing the effect. It is used for the Flying Pigs on page 78. Make a coil using a ⅛in (3mm) wide strip. Glue down the end to make the size of coil you want (see 1). Insert the quilling tool back into the centre and rewind the coil quite firmly – this should bring in the excess paper which gathers at the edge of the strip and creates an ugly 'collar'. As you relax tension on the quilling tool, gently pay out the coil, and encourage the centre of the coil over to the edge (see 2). Hold it in your fingers, then place a small amount of glue on to a smooth surface, such as a tile or piece of cellophane (such as that in a 'window' envelope). Carefully lay the coil on the glue and hold it there until it dries. Gently lift off the coil, which is now ready to use. It can be shaped further, depending on the design (see 3).

Pegs and tight coils

A peg is a tight coil made with a quilling tool (see below). When the end of the strip is reached, it is glued down. A finished peg can be neatened in two ways: by applying pressure to smooth it out, and by inserting a cocktail stick into the centre and twisting to create a neat hole. A tight coil is formed without the use of a quilling tool. The strip is curled over at the very end and rolled tightly on itself so that there is no hole in the centre, and is useful when making faces and snouts (see Flying Pig's nose, page 78).

63

1   2   3

Use this festive tree as a card, or attach a string to the star to make a hanging decoration.

CHRISTMAS TREE PAPERCUT

Materials:

Tracing paper

Pencil

Ivory paper

Coloured paper

Glitter

Glue stick

Tools:

Scalpel (barrel handle and spare blades)

Self-healing cutting mat

Container for blade disposal

Instructions:

1 Photocopy, scan and print, or trace the template opposite onto the paper. Set your work up on a sloped surface such as a tilted drawing board if possible.

2 Start cutting the most difficult section first, or the parts that you feel less confident about, so that if you make a mistake you have not wasted much time. It is usually best to start from the centre and work your way outwards.

3 Take your time, change your blade every 10–15 minutes and take regular breaks to give your hand and neck a rest.

4 Do not worry about rubbing out pencil marks on the back of the paper, as they will not be seen and erasing may damage the paper. You will be working on the reverse of the cut.

5 Resist the temptation to remove the excess paper as you go along. Keeping it in place helps to stabilise the design and you are also less likely to snag the design on your sleeve or jewellery.

6 When complete, cut away the excess paper rather than pushing the design out with your finger, as this will stop it from ripping and you can see if any parts need to be re-cut.

Tip: decorating your tree
Go crazy and fill the bauble circles with different colours. Don't forget the glitter!

Draw around the assembled box to create a triangle-shaped tag. Add a Santa face, as for the box, to create a fun gift tag. Team with a parcel wrapped in plain green paper for a coordinated look.

Beard template: actual size

TREE SANTA GIFT BOX

Materials:

Red, white, flesh-coloured and lime card

White organza ribbon

Red self-adhesive gemstone

Pink chalks

All-purpose glue

3D foam pads

Tools:

Template: beard (opposite) Cricut machine with 'bags, tags, boxes and more' cartridge

Large flower punch

Circle punches, ¾in (2cm), ⅝in (1.3cm) and ¼in (0.5cm)

Small holly die cutter

Ball-tipped embossing stylus and foam mat

Craft knife and cutting mat

Scissors

Instructions:

1 Use a Cricut machine to cut a wedge-shaped box approximately 3 x 2in (7.5 x 5cm) from red card. Alternatively, use a ready-made box or bought template to create the box.

2 Assemble the box and punch holes at either side of the point. Thread through 9¾in (25cm) of ribbon and knot on the inside.

3 Cut two circles of flesh-coloured card ¾in (2cm) and ¼in (0.6cm) in diameter. Using a ball-tipped embossing tool, burnish the small circle (nose) on the back to cup the shape. Punch two tiny holes in the large circle for eyes and add chalk to the cheeks and mouth area.

4 Use the template to cut a beard shape from white card. Also punch a large flower shape and a ⅝in (1.3cm) diameter circle from white card.

5 Cut two petals from the punched white flower and bend to create a moustache. Assemble the face and beard using 3D foam pads. Add a die- or hand-cut holly leaf and gemstone berry.

6 Stick the Santa face to the box using 3D foam pads. Cup the remaining white circle using an embossing tool as for the nose and stick to the box top using a 3D foam pad.

For a Hallowe'en or magic-themed party, transform Santa into Merlin! Cut the box from purple card and add stars cut or punched from iridescent paper. Cut the beard and moustache from grey card to complete the transformation. This design could also be adapted to make three wise men.

QUILLED REINDEER

Instructions:

1 To make the head, make thirty fringed flowers from 4¼in (11cm) strips of ¼in (5mm) mid-brown paper (folowing the instructions on page 63).

2 For the eyes, make two 3in (7.5cm) black pegs (very tight coils), then join on 4¼in (11cm) white strips. Carry on rolling to make an oval shape.

3 For the nose, make a solid coil by rolling up a 17¾in (45cm) red strip with your fingers. Push into a slight dome, coat the underside with glue, then allow to dry.

4 To make the mouth, roll a coil from an 4¼in (11cm) red strip, and pinch into a very thin crescent shape.

5 For the main 'stems' of the antlers, make two very loose coils from 17¾in (45cm) mid-brown strips ⅛in (3mm) wide. Try to distribute the fullness of the paper evenly along the coil, before pinching it into a long, thin slightly curved shape. You may need to put a little glue on the back of the coil to keep the shape from opening up.

6 For the smaller 'branches' of the antlers, make six loose coils from 6in (15cm) mid-brown strips ⅛in (3mm) wide. Again, pinch into slightly curved thin shapes. Make two more coils from 3in (7.5cm) mid-brown strips and shape.

Materials:

Quilling papers: ⅛in (3mm) strips in mid-brown, black, white and red; ¼in (5mm) strips in mid-brown

Beige background card

Brown chalk pastel

Tools:

Quilling tool

Small, sharp scissors

PVA glue

Ruler

7 Make two coils from 6in (15cm) mid-brown strips ⅛in (3mm) wide and pinch at both ends for the ears.

8 To assemble the reindeer, shade the background card with the chalk pastel and then glue down the fringed flowers close together to form the head shape as follows: three flowers on the first three rows; four flowers on the fourth row; five flowers on the fifth and sixth rows; four flowers on the seventh row; and three flowers on the eighth row.

9 Glue on the reindeer's features and then the antlers, beginning with the large 'stem' shapes and then finishing with the smaller 'branches'.

DECOUPAGE CANDLES

Materials:

Three candles of different sizes

Paper napkins with lavender design

Length of lavender organza ribbon

Tools:

Scissors

Two drawing pins or dressmaker's pins

Crafter's heatgun, craft iron or old clothes iron

Instructions:

1 Peel the napkin so you have a single-ply sheet with your chosen image on it.

2 Cut it to fit the size of the candle you are covering, with a very slight overlap at the meeting point.

3 Carefully pin the starting edge of the napkin to the candle just to hold it steady at the start. (You can remove the pins once the tissue starts to adhere to the candle.)

4 Holding the napkin in place, slowly apply heat starting at the edge until the wax begins to melt very slightly. You will see the napkin change colour as the wax begins to seep into it. Do not overheat it and keep the heat source moving or the wax will melt too much and pool into lumps.

5 The edge will be secure now, so remove the pins and start working your way around the candle with the heat source. I used a crafter's heatgun, but if you are using an iron keep it on a very low heat setting.

6 When the candles have cooled, tie all three together with a length of organza ribbon.

WASHI TAPE CARD

Materials:

Washi tape: red paisley, narrow blue

Black solvent inkpad

White and red cardstock

Paper pack

Stickers

Black baker's twine

Black narrow ribbon

Mini white tag

Blank black card 4½ x 6¼in (11.5 x 16cm)

Foam mounting tape

Double-sided tape

Craft glue

Tools:

Small heart stamp

Instructions:

1 Cut a 3¼ x 2½in (8 x 6cm) piece of white cardstock. Place alternating strips of washi tape diagonally, leaving a narrow space between them. Trim off excess tape and ink the edges black. Wrap a piece of narrow black ribbon in the centre.

2 Cut a 3⅜ x ⅞in (8.5 x 2.2cm) piece of red card and ink the edges. Wrap with narrow black ribbon. Use foam tape to attach it to the gift package, making sure the narrow black ribbons match up.

3 Cut a 4⅜ x 3⅜in (11 x 8.5cm) piece of white card and ink the edges. Wrap baker's twine around the top left and bottom right corners. Wrap a short piece of baker's twine

around the piece already at the bottom right and tie it in a knot. Use foam tape to attach the gift package in the centre.

4 Cut a 5½ x 3⅞in (14 x 10cm) piece of green patterned paper and ink the edges. Add a circle sticker in each corner. Mount on white cardstock with double-sided tape and attach to the card front. Use foam tape to attach the white cardstock piece in the centre.

5 Stamp the heart on the tag with black ink. Thread narrow black ribbon through the hole. Foam-tape to the top of the package. Tie a bow in a piece of baker's twine and use craft glue to secure at the top of the tag.

Washi tape gift parcels are great for Christmas. Simply add some metallic shine with gold striped washi tape and gold embroidery thread, then add a candy sweet stamp on the tiny tag for Christmas cheer.

DECOUPAGE DESK TIDY

Materials:

Three clean food cans, labels and adhesive removed

One blank wooden plaque

Chalky finish paints in yellow, pink and green

Paper napkins with flower motifs and butterfly motifs/text

Decoupage glue

Strong metal glue

Tools:

Paintbrushes

Scissors

Instructions:

1 Make sure that the food cans are completely dry and paint the insides with the chalky paint. Use a different colour for each can. Allow the paint to dry completely between coats – two will probably be enough.

2 Now give the outsides of the cans two coats of paint in contrasting colours. Again, allow to dry completely between coats.

3 Carefully peel a paper napkin so that you just have a single-ply piece, and cut out three flower motifs.

4 Using decoupage glue and a paintbrush, carefully apply the flower motif to the food can. The napkin will be very delicate so take your time and stick it down gradually, a section at a time. Carefully encourage the damp napkin to stick to the surface texture of the food can using your paintbrush.

5 Allow the napkin to dry thoroughly before applying a further coat of glue to seal it. Use the decoupage glue to seal the image and the paint on the inside and outside of the food can. Allow the glue to dry well between coats.

6 Paint the plaque using the same colour palette and apply selected images or text to decoupage on the front section.

7 Attach the food cans to the plaque base using some strong metal glue. Alternatively, you may wish to attach them more securely using a drill and some small screws.

RAINY DAY PAPERCUT

Materials:

Tracing paper
Pencil
Ivory paper
Coloured paper
Glue stick

Tools:

Scalpel (barrel handle and spare blades)
Self-healing cutting mat
Container for blade disposal

Tip: adding coloured infills

A rainbow-coloured umbrella will brighten anyone's day. Use pastels or primary colours and tiny dabs of glue on the edge of your knife to apply to the spines of the umbrella – this will help to stick the coloured paper infills in place.

Instructions:

1 Photocopy, scan and print, or trace the template onto the paper. Set your work up on a sloped surface such as a tilted drawing board if possible.

2 Start cutting the most difficult section first, or the parts that you feel less confident about, so that if you make a mistake you have not wasted much time. It is usually best to start from the centre and work your way outwards.

3 Take your time, change your blade every 10–15 minutes and take regular breaks to give your hand and neck a rest.

4 Do not worry about rubbing out pencil marks on the back of the paper, as they will not be seen and erasing may damage the paper. You will be working on the reverse of the cut.

5 Resist the temptation to remove the excess paper as you go along. Keeping it in place helps to stabilise the design and you are also less likely to snag the design on your sleeve or jewellery.

6 When complete, cut away the excess paper rather than pushing the design out with your finger, as this will stop it from ripping and you can see if any parts need to be re-cut.

You can personalise this cheery papercut with your choice of colour for the backing paper and the girl's umbrella.

QUILLED FLYING PIGS

Instructions:

1 To make the head, join a 17¾in (45cm) strip to a 8⅞in (22.5cm) strip in pale peach end to end and make a large coil. Make this into an eccentric circle (see page 63).

2 For the snout, make a tight coil using a 8⅞in (22.5cm) pale peach strip.

3 Join two 17¾in (45cm) pale peach strips end to end and roll into a large coil for the body. Make this into an eccentric circle.

4 For the trotters, make two coils from 6in (15cm) pale peach strips. Pinch into a thin shape rounded at one end. Make a dent at the other end to form the shape of the trotters.

5 Make two coils from 3in (7.5cm) pale peach strips. Form into rounded triangles for the ears.

6 For the wings, make two teardrops from 6in (15cm) white strips, two more from 4¼in (11cm) white strips, and a third pair from 3in (7.5cm) white strips.

7 Roll two pegs from 1¼in (3cm) black strips ¹⁄₁₆in (2mm) wide for the eyes.

8 To assemble, glue the head to the body over the full end of the eccentric circle. Attach the eyes and snout to the head. Draw dots on the snout with a fine black pen. Then glue on both sets of wings, trotters and ears.

9 Make a curly tail by winding a short ¹⁄₁₆in (2mm) strip around a cocktail stick. Trim to size, then glue to the body.

10 For the background, trace the cloud stencil using the template (right) onto a scrap of card, and cut it out. Using this as a guide, move it around the white background card and colour around it with the chalk pastel to make a cloudy sky.

11 To finish, glue down the flying pigs.

Materials:

Quilling papers: ⅛in (3mm) strips in pale peach and white; ¹⁄₁₆in (2mm) strips in black

White background card

Pale blue chalk pastel

Tools:

Quilling tool

Small, sharp scissors

PVA glue

Ruler

Fine black pen

Cocktail stick

Pencil

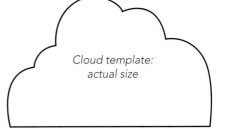

Cloud template: actual size

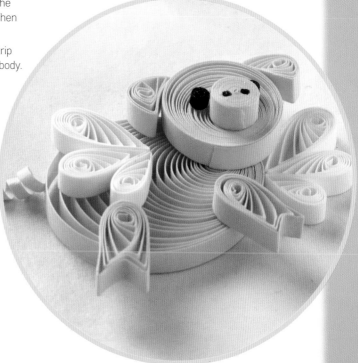

DECOUPAGE CRACKLE MIRROR

Materials:

One square-framed wooden mirror

Black and white patterned decoupage paper

Black or charcoal chalky finish paint

White chalky finish paint

Crackle medium

Decoupage glue

Tools:

Paintbrushes

81

Tip: making your own design
If you can't find any black and white patterned paper that you like, try making your own design with white tissue paper, rubber art stamps and some black ink.

Instructions:

1 Remove the mirror from the wooden frame and set it aside.

2 Paint the frame with a coat of black or charcoal paint and allow it to dry.

3 Apply a coat of crackle medium, making sure that you follow the manufacturer's instructions.

4 When the crackle medium is still slightly tacky and touch dry, apply a coat of white chalky finish paint.

5 Allow the paint to dry naturally and the cracks will appear.

6 Tear pieces from the decoupage paper and glue them to the frame. Because of the nature of decoupage

tissue paper, it will blend into the frame and allow the crackle to show through.

7 Add a few more coats of decoupage glue, allowing each coat to dry before applying the next.

8 When the glue has dried, replace the mirror in the frame.

KNITTING KNOW-HOW

Yarn

Most yarn today comes in hanks or skeins. These are big loops of yarn that are bought by weight and thickness. Before knitting they need to be wound into a ball so that the yarn does not get knotted. Some yarns can be bought ready-prepared as balls. These come in different weights and thicknesses and you can knit directly from them.

There are a variety of yarns used in the projects in this book and these can be substituted for those of your choice. It is advisable to check the length and weight of yarn that you buy against the ones used in the patterns to ensure that you have enough to finish your projects.

Lace yarn (1–3 ply) is a very fine yarn that is used for more open patterns. Generally, you get very long yardage in a 50g ball or hank. Sometimes lighter weight yarns can be doubled to create a more dense look.

Light worsted (DK/8-ply) yarn is a medium thickness yarn that is very versatile and suitable for many projects. This is the most popular weight of yarn.

Worsted (aran/10-ply) yarn is thicker than light worsted (DK/8-ply) yarn and will produce knitted items that are thicker than those made with other weights.

Bulky (chunky) and super bulky (super chunky) weights of yarn are thicker, work up more quickly than lighter weights of yarn and are ideal for bulkier projects.

Knitting needles

Needles are available in metal, plastic and wood. Those made from sustainable wood are very comfortable to work with, extremely durable and flexible to work with in all temperatures.

For some of the projects you will need cable needles or circular needles. Many people find that the yarns stay on needles made from sustainable wood better than metal or plastic needles. Experiment to find out what suits you best.

Other items

For all of the projects you will need a pair of good-quality, sharp scissors to cut off the ends of yarns when sewing them into your work.

As well as knitting needles, you will also need a blunt-ended needle with a large eye, such as a tapestry needle, for sewing up all your projects and weaving in any loose ends. You may also need a sewing or embroidery needle and sewing or embroidery thread for some projects.

A tape measure and stitch markers are useful tools to have to hand.

You will also need small amounts of toy stuffing for the Twinkling Star (page 88), Holly Christmas Bear (page 94), the Knitted Pear (page 100), the Christmas Holly Cake (page 104), the Pumpkin (page 108), the Christmas Tree (page 120) and the Rocking Robin (page 128).

Beads, buttons, bells, ribbon and sequins (or sequin yarn) are also great embellishments for some projects and are listed with individual patterns if needed.

Gauge (tension)

Some projects, such as garments or other items that need to be a particular size (such as tea cosies), will require you to work to a specific gauge (tension). Details of this are included with the relevant pattern. It is a good idea in such cases to knit a gauge (tension) swatch to the manufacturer's guidelines of 4 x 4in (10 x 10cm) in stockinette stitch (UK stocking stitch); these swatches will also be helpful if you decide to use alternative yarns to those used in the projects.

The Red Rooster Scarf uses an attractive double cable pattern (see page 126).

There are a number of simple knitting techniques that come in very handy for things such as joining your pieces together and making up your projects. Those below are the most frequently used in this book.

Making up

Many of the projects are sewn together using a darning or tapestry needle and the same yarn the item has been knitted in. If any other needles (for example, a sewing needle) are required, they are listed with the individual patterns.

Mattress stitch

Mattress stitch makes a practically invisible and nicely flexible seam for joining pieces together. Several of the projects use it, such as the Snowflake Headband (page 86) and the Crystal Phone Sock (page 106).

1 With the right sides of the work facing, start with your yarn in the lower right corner. Take your tapestry needle across to the left edge and under the strand of yarn between the first and second stitches of the first row.

2 Take your needle back to the right edge and insert it one row up, between the first and second stitches of the row.

3 Take your needle back to the left edge and repeat stages one and two.

4 After completing a few stitches, gently pull the long end of the yarn to draw the stitches together, making your seam virtually invisible.

Blanket stitch

Thread a darning needle with yarn and bring to the front of your work about ⅜in (1cm) from the edge. Leaving a small gap along the edge of the work, take the needle to the back of the work approximately ⅜in (1cm) in from the edge and bring it back to the front at the edge of the knitting. Loop your yarn under the needle and pull it through until it lays neatly against the emerging yarn. Repeat this process.

Running stitch

This is a simple embroidery stitch that is very useful for surface decoration. Thread your sewing needle and begin by bringing your thread up from the underside of the material or knitted work, then taking the needle back down, leaving a space from the beginning of your work. Continue in this manner, making sure that the spaces between your stitches are even.

I-cord

I-cords are very useful when you need to make long, thin pieces of knitting, such as Rocking Robin's legs (see below and page 128). To make an i-cord, cast on your stitches using a double-pointed needle, knit them and slide them to the other end of the same needle, then pull the yarn across the back of the needle and knit the stitches again. Repeat these instructions until the cord is long enough. By pulling the yarn behind the stitches on the needle, you close the 'gap' and give the appearance of French knitting. Alternatively, you can work the stitches in stockinette stitch (UK stocking stitch) and sew up the seam.

French knots

French knots are a simple way of providing very attractive surface decoration. They can be used to make flowers, eyes, or simple bobble shapes. If you are making Holly Christmas Bear (see page 94) for a young child, for example, and do not want to use toy safety eyes or beads, you can make the eyes using French knots.

Bring the needle up from the back of the work through to the front and wind the yarn around the needle twice. Take the needle through the work, half a stitch away, holding the loops around the needle with your finger while pulling the yarn through to the back of your work. Fasten off.

Abbreviations

Many common knitting abbreviations used in this book are listed in the table below.

alt:	alternate		rem:	remaining
cm:	centimetres		rep:	repeat
dec:	decrease		RS:	right side
DPN:	double-pointed needles		skpo:	slip 1, knit 1, pass slipped stitch over
foll:	following		sl:	slip a stitch
GS:	garter stitch (knit every row)		SM:	slip marker from left to right needle
in	inches		st st:	stockinette stitch (UK stocking stitch) – alternate knit and purl rows
inc:	increase (by working into the front and back of the stitch)		ssk:	slip 2 sts knitwise one at a time, pass the two slipped sts back to left needle, knit both together through the back of the loop
K:	knit			
Kfb:	knit into the front and back of the stitch (increasing one stitch)		ssp:	slip 2 sts knitwise one at a time, pass two slipped sts back to left needle, purl two slipped sts together from the back, left to right
K2tog:	knit 2 stitches together			
M:	marker		st(s):	stitch(es)
M1:	make a backwards loop on your needle by twisting the yarn towards you and slipping the resulting loop on to the right-hand needle. On the following row knit or purl through the back of the st.		tbl:	through the back of the loop
			tog:	together
			W&T:	wrap and turn
			WS:	wrong side
P:	purl		YO:	yarn over needle, resulting in another stitch
PM:	place marker			
P2tog:	purl 2 stitches together			
psso:	pass slipped stitch over			

This headband will complement any winter outfit in these soft, neutral colours.

SNOWFLAKE HEADBAND

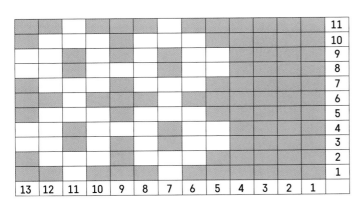

Materials:

2 balls of DK (8-ply) merino/alpaca yarn – 1 x slate grey (A), 1 x ivory (B), each 50g/113m/124yd

Needles:

1 pair of 4mm (UK 8, US 6) knitting needles

1 stitch marker

87

Instructions:

Using size 4mm (UK 8, US 6) needles and colour A, cast on 108 sts, then ktbl to form a neat edge.

Rows 1 and 2: *k1, p1, rep from * to end.

Row 3: *k3B, k1A, rep from * to end.

Row 4: p2B, *p1A, p3B, rep from * to last 2 sts, p1A, p1B.

Row 5: knit in A.

Row 6: purl in A.

Row 7: Work chart row 1 eight times across row in knit, k4A.

Continue working from the chart; odd-numbered rows are knitted and worked from right to left, and even-numbered rows are purled working from left to right.

Next row: purl in A.

Next row: knit in A.

Next row: *p1A, p3B, rep from * to end.

Next row: k1B, *k1A, k3B, rep from * to last 3 sts, k1A, k2B.

Cut off yarn B.

Next row: purl.

Next row: knit.

Work next 2 rows as rows 1 and 2 of pattern.

Cast off.

Making up
With RS facing, join seams together using mattress stitch. Weave in all loose ends.

Make other stars in silver and you have a starry firmament of Christmas decorations for the tree or around the house.

TWINKLING STAR

Materials:

Small amount of fingering (4-ply) yarn
in gold

Small amount of fingering (4-ply)
sequin yarn

Spare needle/stitch holder

Toy stuffing

Needles:

1 pair of 3.25mm (UK 10, US 3) knitting
needles

Spare needle or stitch holder

Size:

Approx. 3⅛in (8cm) across from point to point

Instructions:

Star points (make five)

Holding a strand of gold fingering (4-ply) yarn and a strand
of sequin yarn together, cast on 2 sts and knit 2 rows.

Next row: k1, M1, k1 (3 sts).

K 2 rows.

Next row: k1, k1fb, k1 (4 sts).

K 1 row.

Next row: k2, M1, k2 (5 sts).

K 1 row.

Next row: k2, k1fb, k2 (6 sts).

Place sts of each point on a spare needle or stitch holder.

Centre of star

With RS facing, k across all five points of the star (30 sts).

Next row: (k1, k2tog) to end of row (20 sts).

K1 row.

Next row: k2tog to end of row (10 sts).

K1 row.

Thread yarn through rem sts and draw up, fasten off and
sew side seam of star.

Make a second star shape in the same way.

Making up

With WS together, sew the stars carefully together, folding
all the loose ends into the inside of the star and filling
gently with toy stuffing as you go.

I knitted a smaller version, measuring 7¾ x 2¾in (20 x 7cm), by following the same pattern but using red fingering (4-ply) yarn and size 3.25mm (UK 10; US 3) needles. I stitched a gold star button into the centre of each square.

SNOWFLAKES MUG HUG

Materials:

1 ball of light worsted (DK/8-ply)
  knitting yarn in dark blue;
  50g/137yd/125m

7 white snowflake buttons

1 plain blue button

Needles:

1 pair of 4mm (UK 8, US 6) knitting needles

Size:

9 x 3¼in (23 x 8cm)

Instructions:

Cast on 7 sts.

Knit 2 rows.

Continue in GS.

Inc 1 st at each end of next and every alt row until 19 sts on needle.

Proceed in GS and block pattern as follows:

Row 1: knit.

Row 2: k3, p6, k to end.

Rows 3–8: rep rows 1 and 2 three times.

Rows 9–11: knit.

Row 12: knit to last 9 sts, p6, k3.

Rows 13–18: rep rows 11 and 12, 3 times.

Row 19–20: knit.

Rep rows 1–20 twice, then rep rows 1–10 once.

Continue in GS and shape buttonhole end:

Dec 1 st at each end of next and every alt row until 11 sts on needle.

Next row: to make buttonhole, k2tog, k3, yo, k2tog, knit to last 2 sts, k2tog.

Next row: knit, knitting into yrn of previous row.

Continue to dec as before until 7 sts rem.

Knit 2 rows.

Cast off.

Making up

Work in all ends neatly. Sew the snowflake buttons into the squares, as shown in the photograph below. Sew the blue button on to the end of the mug hug to correspond with the buttonhole at the other end.

Everyone loves snowmen. I have knitted the motif using intarsia to avoid large loops at the back of the work, and cut-off lengths of white and black yarn to make the knitting easier.

FROSTY WRIST WARMERS

Materials:
3 balls of light worsted (DK/8-ply) merino yarn – 1 x red (A),
1 x white (B), 1 x black (C); 100g/273yd/250m

Needles:
1 pair of 4mm (UK 8, US 6)
knitting needles

Instructions:

Make two.

The black yarn is used double throughout to accentuate the snowman's hat and buttons.

Using yarn A, cast on 40 sts, then ktbl to form a neat edge.

Rows 1–16: *k1, p1*, rep from * to * to end of row.

Rows 17–18: st st.

Row 19: k2A, *k1B, k4A*, rep from * to * to last pattern rep, k2A.

Row 20: p1A, *p3B, p2A*, rep from * to * to last pattern rep, p1A.

Row 21: *k2B, k1A, k2B*, rep from * to * to end of row.

Row 22: As row 20.

Row 23: As row 19. Cut off yarn B.

Rows 24–26: st st in yarn A.

Row 27: Work row 1 of the chart, placing the 2 snowmen motifs as follows: k7A, k7B, k12A, k7B, k7A to set the spacing, then continue to work rows 2–26 from chart. Cut off yarns B and C.

Next 2 rows: st st, using yarn A.

Next 2 rows: *k1, p1*, rep to end of row.

Cast off all sts.

Making up
With RS facing, use a tapestry needle and mattress stitch to join the side seams, 4in (10cm) from the wrist end and 2in (5cm) from the finger end. This will leave a gap for your thumb to go through.

Weave in all loose ends.

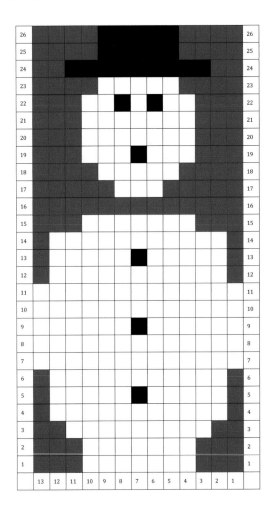

HOLLY CHRISTMAS BEAR

Materials:

1 ball each of light worsted (DK/8-ply) yarn in beige, red and sparkly white; 50g/137yd/125m

Small quantity of toy stuffing

Two 6mm round black beads for eyes

Black embroidery thread or floss for features

Strong thread for sewing

3 gold star buttons

1 candle button

39½in (1m) red satin ribbon, ¼in (5mm) wide

Tools:

1 pair 3.25mm (UK 10, US 3) knitting needles

Sewing needle

Stitch holder

Instructions

Work the bear entirely in GS, unless otherwise stated.

Bear's head

Cast on 30 sts.

Rows 1–4: GS.

Row 5: k2, skpo, knit to last 3 sts, K2tog, k1.

Rows 6–7: GS.

Continue to dec in this way on every third row until 8 sts rem.

Next row: k2, skpo, k2tog, k2.

Next row: k2, skpo, k2.

Next row: k1, sl1, k2tog, psso, k1.

Next row: k3tog.

Fasten off.

Body and legs (make 2 pieces the same)

Cast on 12 sts.

Rows 1–2: GS.

Rows 3–8: inc 1 st at each end of rows 3, 5 and 7 (18 sts).

Rows 8–33: knit.

Row 34: divide for legs; k8, cast-off 2, knit to end (8 sts).

Proceed on these 8 sts for first leg.

Rows 35–52: knit.

Row 53: k2tog, knit to last 2 sts, k2tog.

Row 54: cast off.

Return to stitches left on needle, rejoin yarn and complete to match first leg.

Arms (make 2)

Cast on 6 sts.

Row 1: knit.

Row 2: knit twice into each st to end (12 sts).

Rows 3–6: knit.

Row 7: inc 1 st at each end of row (14 sts).

Rows 8–27: knit.

Rows 28–30: dec 1 st at each end of rows 28 and 30 (10 sts).

Row 31: k2, (k2tog) three times, k2 (7 sts).

Row 32: knit.

Cast off (this is the top of the arm).

Making up

Make up the head by folding the three corners of the triangle into the centre; the fold lines are shown in the top diagram opposite. Sew the two side seams either side of the nose, and across the corner lines to form the ears, as shown in the lower diagram.

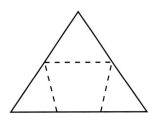

Sew a little way along the neck seam, just down from the nose. Stuff the head firmly to give it a good shape. Stitch on the nose and mouth with black thread, and sew on the eyes.

Stitch the back and front body pieces together using a flat seam on the right side of the work. Leave the neck edge open for stuffing. Stuff firmly and then close the neck opening. Attach the head to the body.

Dress

Bodice front

Using red yarn, cast on 24 sts.

Rows 1–6: st st.

Rows 7–8: cast off 2 sts at beg of each row.

Rows 9–10: st st.

Row 11: dec 1 st at each end of row (18 sts).

Row 12: purl.

Rows 13–16: st st.

Divide for neck:

Work 7 sts, slip next 4 sts on to stitch holder, work 7 sts.

Continue on first 7 sts for side of neck.

Dec 1 st at neck edge on next and following alt rows until 4 sts rem.

Cast off.

Work other side to match.

Bodice back

Work rows 1–16 of bodice front.

Rows 17–21: st st.

Cast off.

Skirt

With RS facing, pick up and knit 24 sts along cast-on edge of bodice front.

Next row: purl.

Next row: knit twice into each st (48 sts).

Continue in st st and when skirt measures 2¼in (6cm), change to white yarn.

Work 3 rows GS.

Repeat the above, on bodice back.

Cast off.

Neckband

Using white yarn, join one shoulder seam.

With RS facing, pick up and knit 5 sts down one side of neck, 4 sts from stitch holder across front of neck, 5 sts up other side of neck and 10 sts around back of neck (rem 4 sts will form other shoulder).

Next row: knit.

Cast off knitwise.

Sleeves (make two)

Using white, cast on 24 sts.

Rows 1–2: knit.

Break yarn and join in red.

Rows 3–10: st st.

Cast off.

Boots

Using red yarn, cast on 14 sts.

Next row: knit.

Next row: inc in each st across row (28 sts).

Work 5 rows GS.

Next row: k2tog, K8, (k2tog) 4 times, kk8, k2tog.

Next row: K9, (k2tog) twice, K9.

Next row: knit.

Cast off.

For tops of boots, cast on 16 sts in white and knit 2 rows.

Cast off.

Stitch the seam along the base and back of the shoe. Put a tiny amount of stuffing inside the shoe, place the base of the leg inside the shoe and stitch it in place. Sew on the gold star buttons.

Muff

Using white, cast on 18 sts.

Rows 1–2: GS.

Join in red yarn.

Rows 3–12: st st, ending with a purl row.

Rows 13–14: GS, using white yarn.

Cast off.

Hat

Using white, cast on 36 sts.

Rows 1–10: GS.

Break white yarn and join in red.

Rows 11–16: st st.

To shape top of hat:

Row 17: (k4, skpo) across row (30 sts).

Rows 18–20: st st.

Row 21: (k3, skpo) across row (24 sts).

Row 22: purl.

Row 23: (k2, skpo) across row (18 sts).

Row 24: purl.

Row 25: k2tog across row (9 sts).

Break yarn and thread through rem sts. Pull tight and fasten off.

Making up

Sew the side seams of the dress and turn right-side out. Slip the dress on to the bear. Catch together the neckband and shoulder seam neatly. Sew the sleeve seams then stitch the sleeves to the armholes.

Stitch the side seam of the muff, roll it into a cylinder shape and attach the star button to the front. Cut a length of ribbon long enough to form a strap and stitch it inside the muff, making sure the ribbon join is hidden inside. Join the side seam of the hat and turn back the brim. Make a tiny pom-pom and sew it to the top of the hat. Place the hat on the bear's head and secure. Sew the candle button on the front.

BOBBLE SCARF

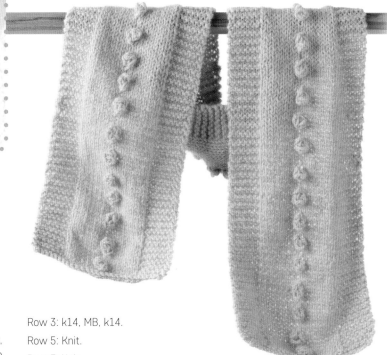

Instructions:

Bobble

To make bobble [MB]: (k1, yo, k1, yo, k1) into next stitch, turn and p5, turn and k1, sl1, k2tog, psso, k1, turn and p3tog.

When you have made the bobble, turn and knit into the bobble st again in the main colour and then continue knitting across the row.

Initial rows

Rows 1–2: Using 7mm (UK 2, US 10½) needles, cast on 29sts in mist grey, then ktbl on return row (i.e. row 2).

Main scarf pattern

Row 1: Knit.

Row 2 and all even rows: k7, p15, k7.

Row 3: k14, MB, k14.

Row 5: Knit.

Row 7: Knit.

Row 9: As row 3, MB.

Row 11: Knit.

Row 12: As row 2.

Continue with this twelve-row pattern ten times more and then repeat rows 1–11.

Next row: As row 2. Cast off.

Making up

Weave in loose ends on the WS of your work.

The same yarn in pale yellow makes the perfect partner for the green pear.

KNITTED PEAR

Materials:

1 ball of light worsted (DK/8-ply) cotton yarn in pale green; 50g/137yd/125m

Toy stuffing

Tapestry needle

Needles:

Set of four 3.25mm (UK 10, US 3) DPN

Size:

4in (12cm) high, excluding the stalk

Instructions:

Pear (make 1)

With size 3.25mm (UK 10, US 3) double-pointed knitting needles and pale green yarn, cast on 12 sts and divide between three needles.

Round 1: k.

Round 2: inc1 in each st (24 sts).

Round 3: k.

Round 4: (inc1, k1) 12 times (36 sts).

Rounds 5–7: k.

Round 8: (inc1, k2) 12 times (48 sts).

Rounds 9–20: k.

Round 21: (k2tog, k2) 12 times (36 sts).

Rounds 22–27: k.

Round 28: (k2tog, k1) 12 times (24 sts).

Rounds 29–33: k.

Round 34: (k2tog) 12 times (12 sts).

Rounds 35–36: k.

Round 37: (k2tog) 6 times.

Cut yarn and thread through rem 6 sts; fasten off.

Stalk (make 1)

Using brown yarn, cast on 3 sts.

Row 1: k3; do not turn but slide sts to other end of needle.

Rep row 1 until cord measures 1¾in (4cm); cut yarn, leaving a tail. Fasten off.

Making up

Fill the pear with toy stuffing, then pull the yarn to close the stitches on the last row, inserting one end of the stalk as you do so. Secure the stalk with one or two discreet stitches, then thread the tail of the yarn in and out of the last two stitches to create a knobbly end to the stalk. With spare brown yarn, embroider a small star on the base of the pear (see detail, below).

Penguins are always fun to work with and these cuffs will liven up any boots. This pattern is suitable for a knitter who has mastered the basics. To change the look, try knitting them in different colours.

PENGUIN BOOT CUFFS

Materials:

2 balls each of light worsted (DK/8-ply) pure alpaca yarn in pale turquoise (A) and 1 ball each in gold (B), mid-blue (C) and cream (D); 50g/109yd/100m

Needles:

1 pair of 5mm (UK 6, US 8) knitting needles

Instructions:

Make two.

Cast on 58sts in yarn A.

Knit into the back of the sts to form a neat edge.

Using the chart place pattern as follows:

Even row numbers are knit and odd numbers are purl.

Row 1: k2A, *3B, 2A, 3B, 6A* rep from * to * three times more.

Continue working from the chart until row 18. Cut off yarn C. The rest of the knitting is done in yarn A.

Row 19: knit.

Row 20: purl.

Now continue in ribbing.

Ribbing

Row 1: *k2, p2* rep until the last two sts, k2.

Row 2: *p2, k2* rep until the last two sts, p2.

Rows 3–20: Rep rows 1 and 2 nine more times.

Row 21: As row 1.

Row 22: Cast off sts.

Making up

Use a tapestry needle to sew in loose ends by weaving them into stitches at the back of your work.

With RS facing, use a mattress stitch to join the side seams of the pattern component of the boot cuff.

Sew up the rib on the rear side of the boot cuff.

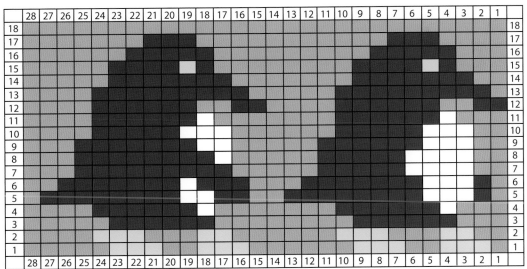

The holly and berries have been replaced by a charming Christmas rose on this alternative version of the domed Christmas holly cake (above left). The rose is knitted using the flower pattern below. Small holly-shaped beads have been used to decorate the cake.

Christmas rose for alternative cake

Cast on 8 sts using white yarn. Work in st st.

Row 1: knit.

Row 2: purl.

Row 3: knit, increasing every st (16 sts).

Row 4: purl.

Row 5: knit, increasing every st (32 sts).

Row 6: purl.

Row 7: knit, increasing every st (64 sts).

Cast off in purl.

CHRISTMAS HOLLY CAKE

Instructions:

Top of cake

Cast on 51 sts using white wool and double-ended needles – 17 sts on each of 3 needles.

Rounds 1–26: knit.

Round 27: * dec 2 sts randomly on each needle * (15 sts on each needle).

Rounds 28–33: repeat from * to * (3 sts on each needle).

Round 34: K2tog, K1 (2 sts on each needle).

Break yarn, leaving a long end. Thread through stitches on needles and draw up tightly.

Base of cake

Cast on 12 sts using white wool and 2.5mm (US 2, UK 12) needles and work in st st.

Row 1: ** purl.

Row 2: knit, increasing 1 st at beg and end of row. **

Rows 3–8: repeat from ** to ** (20 sts).

Rows 9–11: continue in st st.

Rows 12–18: dec 1 st at beg and end of every k row (12 sts).

Row 19: purl.

Cast off.

Holly (make 2 leaves)

Cast on 2 sts using green wool and 3.25mm (US 3, UK 10) needles.

Rows 1–2: work in st st, starting with a K row.

Row 3: inc both sts (4 sts).

Rows 4–6: st st.

Row 7: inc first and last st (6 sts).

Row 8: purl.

Row 9: inc first and last st (8 sts).

Row 10: purl.

Row 11: K2tog at beg and end of row (6 sts).

Row 12: purl.

Row 13: repeat row 11 (4 sts).

Row 14: purl.

Row 15: k2tog, k2tog.

Row 16: p2tog.

Berries

Make 3 berries.

Cast on 5 sts using red wool and 3.25mm (US 3, UK 10) needles.

Rows 1–5: st st.

Cast off.

Making up

Pull up the thread at the top of the cake holding the remaining stitches, then darn the thread end into the stitches at the back of the knitting. Stuff the domed cake with toy stuffing then stitch it on to the cake base. Wrap a length of ribbon around the cake, overlapping the ends before stitching it in place. Make a row of gathering stitching around the edge of the knitted berry. Add a small amount of toy stuffing to the centre, then pull up the thread and secure. Stitch the holly leaves and the berries to the top of the cake.

CRYSTAL PHONE SOCK

Instructions:

Front

Using 3.5mm (UK 10/9, US 4) needles, cast on 19 sts in red.

Rows 1–6: st st, starting with a knit row.

Begin pattern:

Row 1: k6(R), k1(W), k5(R), k1(W), k6(R).

Row 2: p6(R), p2(W), p3(R), p2(W), p6(R).

Row 3: k6(R), k3(W), k1(R), k3(W), k6(R).

Row 4: p6(R), p3(W), p1(R), p3(W), p6(R).

Row 5: k2(R), k4(W), k1(R), k2(W), k1(R), k2(W), k1(R), k4(W), k2(R).

Row 6: p3(R), p4(W), p1(R), p1(W), p1(R), p1(W), p1(R), p4(W), p3(R).

Row 7: k4(R), k4(W), k3(R), k4(W), k4(R).

Row 8: p9(R), p1(W), p9(R).

Row 9: k4(R), k4(W), k3(R), k4(W), k4(R).

Row 10: p3(R), p4(W), p1(R), p1(W), p1(R), p1(W), p1(R), p4(W), p3(R).

Row 11: k2(R), k4(W), k1(R), k2(W), k1(R), k2(W), k1(R), k4(W), k2(R).

Materials:

1 ball of light worsted (DK/8-ply) yarn in red (R) and a small amount in white (W); 50g/137yd/125m

Tools:

1 pair 3.5mm (UK 10/9, US 4) knitting needles

1 pair 3.25mm (UK 10, US 3) knitting needles

Tapestry needle

Scissors

Tape measure

Row 12: p6(R), p3(W), p1(R), p3(W), p6(R).

Row 13: k6(R), k3(W), k1(R), k3(W), k6(R).

Row 14: p6(R), p2(W), p3(R), p2(W), p6(R).

Row 15: k6(R), k1(W), k5(R), k1(W), k6(R).

Rows 16–24: st st in red, starting and finishing with a purl row.

Row 25: Join in white, k1(R), k1(W) to end of row.

Row 26: p1(W), p1(R) to end of row.

Row 27: k1(R), k1(W) to end of row.

Row 28: change to 3.35mm (UK 10, US 3) needles and rib for 2in (5cm).

Cast off.

Back

Using 3.5mm (UK 10/9, US 4) needles, cast on 19 sts and work st st for 4¼in (11cm) in red.

Next row: Join in white, k1(R), k1(W) to end of row.

Next row: p1(W), p1(R) to end of row.

Next row: k1(R), k1(W) to end of row.

Change to 3.25mm (UK 10, US 3) needles and rib for 2in (5cm).

Cast off.

Making up

Close the side seams using mattress stitch.

PUMPKIN

Instructions:

Pumpkin

With set of five 3.25mm (UK 10, US 3) DPN and orange yarn, cast on 16 sts and distribute these equally between four needles.

Round 1: k.

Round 2: (inc1, k1) eight times (24 sts).

Round 3: (inc1, k1, p1) eight times (32 sts).

Round 4: (inc1, k2, p1) eight times (40 sts).

Round 5: (inc1, k3, p1) eight times (48 sts).

Round 6: (inc1, k4, p1) eight times (56 sts).

Round 7: (inc1, k5, p1) eight times (64 sts).

Round 8: (inc1, k6, p1) eight times (72 sts).

Round 9: (k8, p1) 8 times.

Rounds 10–19: Rep round 9.

Round 20: (k7, k2tog) eight times (64 sts).

Round 21: (k6, k2tog) eight times (56 sts).

Round 22: (k5, k2tog) eight times (48 sts).

Round 23: (k4, k2tog) eight times (40 sts).

Round 24: (k3, k2tog) eight times (32 sts).

Round 25: (k2, k2tog) eight times (24 sts).

Round 26: (k1, k2tog) eight times (16 sts).

Round 27: k2tog eight times.

Break yarn and thread through rem 8 sts.

Stalk

With green yarn and pair of size 3.25 mm (UK 10, US 3) needles, cast on 2 sts.

Row 1: k both sts tbl.

Row 2 and every even-numbered row: k.

Row 3: cast on 2, k to end (4 sts).

Row 5: cast on 3, k to end (7 sts).

Row 7: cast off 3, k to end (4 sts).

Row 9: cast off 2, k to end (2 sts).

Row 10: k.

Rows 11–34: Rep rows 3–10 three times.

Rows 35–36: Rep rows 1–9 (2 sts).

Row 37: cast on 6 sts, k to end (8 sts).

Rows 38–44: k.

Cast off and break yarn, leaving a long tail.

Making up

Pull up the stitches on the last row of the pumpkin and fasten off securely; this forms the base of the pumpkin. Insert stuffing through the hole formed by the cast-on edge. Fill the pumpkin fairly tightly but do not over-stuff or it will become stretched out of shape. Thread a tapestry needle with orange yarn, then thread through stitches around the hole in the top of the pumpkin and pull up. Roll up the stalk and, with the tail of green yarn, stitch the side edges of the stalk and leaves together, then stitch the stalk to the top of the pumpkin.

Simply adjust the pattern if you want to move or substitute any of the colours given here.

STRIPES TEA COSY

Instructions:

Make two.

Using cream yarn, cast on 42 sts.

Work 12 rows in SS.

Change to navy yarn and work 6 rows.

Change to cream yarn and work 6 rows.

Change to yellow yarn and work 6 rows.

Change to cream yarn and work 6 rows.

Change to red yarn and work 6 rows.

Change to cream yarn and work 6 rows.

Change to turquoise yarn and work 2 rows.

Shape the top

Row 1: continue with turquoise yarn, k7, k2tog, *k6, k2tog*, rep from * to * to last st, k1.

Row 2: purl.

Row 3: k6, k2tog, *k5, k2tog*, rep from * to * to last st, k1.

Row 4: purl.

Row 5: change to cream yarn and k5, k2tog, *k4, k2tog*, rep from * to * to last st, k1.

Row 6: purl.

Row 7: k4, k2tog, *k3, k2tog*, rep from * to * to last st, k1.

Row 8: purl.

Row 9: k3, k2tog, *k2, k2tog*, rep from * to * to last st, k1.

Row 10: purl.

Row 11: k2, k2tog, *k1, k2tog*, rep from * to * to last st, k1.

Row 12: purl.

Row 13: change to navy yarn and k1, k2tog, *k2tog*, rep from * to * to last st, k1.

Row 14: purl.

Row 15: knit.

Row 16: purl.

Row 17: knit.

Cut yarn and place sts on stitch holder.

Make up the cosy

Place the wrong sides of the cosy together (RS facing out).

Thread tapestry needle with the navy tail on the back stitch holder.

Graft the sts on the stitch holders together.

Sew the top

Continue sewing with the tail down one side for 4in (10cm).

Fasten off and hide tail in the seam.

Repeat on other side of cosy.

Sew the bottom

Thread the tapestry needle with one of the cream tails of yarn from the cast on edge.

Sew up one side for 1½in (4cm).

Fasten off and hide tail in the seam.

Repeat on the other side of cosy.

PERIWINKLE

113

Materials:

Small amounts of fingering (4-ply) yarn in blue and ivory

Glass seed beads, yellow

Sewing thread, white or yellow

Needles:

1 pair of 2.25mm (UK 13, US 1) knitting needles

Tapestry needle

Stitch holder

Sewing needle

Size:

2¾in (7cm) across

Instructions:

Petal (make 5)

Cast on 12 sts using blue yarn.

Row 1: (k1, sl 1 purlwise with yarn at back of work) six times.

Rep last row 15 times; break off yarn.

Join in ivory yarn and rep row 1 six times more.

Break off yarn, leaving a long tail; transfer to a stitch holder.

Making up

Each petal needs to be finished off before joining to make up the flower. Thread the tail of yarn on to a tapestry needle. Carefully slip stitches off the stitch holder and pull apart the two sides of the petal, separating the stitches. Thread the yarn through each stitch in turn then turn the petal inside out and pull up the yarn to gather the base of the petal.

Join the petals at the centre, then sew on a little cluster of eight seed beads.

Alpaca yarn creates a really soft fabric that stretches beautifully – but you could substitute your own choice of yarn as long as it knits to the same gauge (tension).

BOW BEANIE

Instructions:

Band
Cast on 30 sts.

Row 1 (WS): (p3, k3) five times.

Rep row 1 160 times.

Cast off, leaving 1 st on needle; do not cut the yarn.

Crown
With RS facing, pick up and knit 126 sts along the long edge of the band, inc. st. on needle.

Row 1 (WS): (p3, k3) 21 times.

Rep row 1 17 times.

Row 19: (p3, p2tog, p1) 21 times (105 sts).

Row 20: (p2, k3) 21 times.

Row 21: (p3,k2) 21 times.

Row 23: (p3, p2tog) 21 times (84 sts).

Row 24: (p1, k3) 21 times.

Row 25: (p3,k1) 21 times.

Row 26: (p1, k3) 21 times.

Row 27: (p3,k1) 21 times.

Row 28: k1, (sl1, k2tog, psso, k5) 10 times, sl1, k2tog, psso (62 sts).

Row 29: purl.

Row 30: k1, (sl1, k2tog, psso, k3) 10 times, p1 (42 sts).

Row 31: purl.

Row 32: k1, (sl1, k2tog, psso, k1) 10 times, p1 (22 sts).

Row 33: purl.

Row 34: k1, (k2tog) 10 times, k1 (12 sts).

Row 35: (p2tog) 6 times.

Cut yarn and thread tail through rem 6 sts.

Materials:
2 balls of light worsted (DK/8-ply) alpaca yarn in pink; 50g/137yd/125m

Needles:
3.75mm (UK 9, US 5) knitting needles

Tapestry needle

Gauge/tension:
30 sts and 29 rows to 4in (10cm), measured over rib pattern, using 3.75mm (UK 9, US 5) knitting needles, (measured without stretching)

Size:
To fit an average adult female head

Bow
Cast on 21 sts.

Row 1 (RS): (k3, p3) 3 times, k3.

Row 2: (p3, k3) 3 times, p3.

Rep rows 1 and 2 48 times.

Cast off.

Centre
Cast on 6 sts.

Row 1 (RS): knit.

Row 2: purl.

Rep rows 1 and 2 24 times.

Cast off.

Making up
Pull up the tail of yarn to gather the stitches on top of the crown and secure then, with right sides together and using the tail of yarn, stitch up the seam in backstitch. On the band, pull up the stitches of the seam to gather the short ends together. Stitch the short ends of the bow together, then wrap the centre piece around the join. Stitch the bow to the band, lining up the centre of the bow with the gathered part of the band.

Materials:

1 ball of fingering (4-ply) baby yarn in
  green; 50g/191yd/175m

1 ball of fingering (4-ply) baby yarn in
  red; 50g/191yd/175m

Oddments of fingering (4-ply) baby
  yarn in yellow and white

Needles:

1 pair 3.75mm (UK 9, US 5)
  knitting needles

BERRY BOOTEES

Instructions:

Make two

Using green yarn, cast on 37 sts.
Rows 1–5: GS. Break green yarn.
Join in red.
Rows 6–9: st st.
Join in yellow.
Row 10: k4 red, k1 yellow, *k3 red, k1 yellow*, rep from * to * to last 4 sts, K4 red.
Rows 11–15: using red, work 5 rows in st st, beg with a purl row.
Row 16: k2 red, *k1 yellow, k3 red*, rep from * to * to last 3 sts, k1 yellow, k2 red.
Rows 17–21: using red, work 5 rows in st st, beg with a purl row.
Row 22: k4 red, k1 yellow, *k3 red, k1 yellow*, rep from * to * to last 4 sts, k4 red.
Rows 23–25: using red, work 3 rows in st st, beg with a purl row.
Join in green yarn.

Shape instep as follows:
Row 26: k13 green, k11 red.
Turn and work on these 11 sts for instep.
Row 27: purl in red.
Row 28: k3 red, k1 yellow, k3 red, k1 yellow, k3 red.
Rows 29–33: using red, work 5 rows in SS, beg with a purl row.
Row 34: k5 red, k1 yellow, k5 red.
Rows 35–39: using red, work 5 rows in SS, beg with a purl row.
Row 40: k3 red, K1 yellow, K3 red, k1 yellow, k3 red.
Row 41: purl in red.
Break red.
With right sides facing and using green yarn, pick up and knit 10 sts along first side of instep, 11 sts from instep, 10 sts down other side of instep, and knit across rem 13 sts (57 sts).

Work 15 rows in GS.
Shape foot as follows:
Next row: k1, * k2togtbl, k23, k2tog, k1*, rep from * to * to end of row.
Next row: knit.
Next row: k1, * k2togtbl, k21, K2tog, k1*, rep from * to * to end of row.
Next row: knit.
Next row: k1, *k2togtbl, k19, k2tog, k1*, rep from * to * to end of row.
Next row: knit.
Cast off.

Strap

Make two.
Using green yarn, cast on 4 sts.
Work 36 rows in GS. Cast off.

Flowers

Make two.
Using white yarn, cast on 30 sts.
Row 1: k1, *cast off next 4 sts (1 st rem on needle), k1*, rep from * to * to end of row.
Break yarn and run through sts on needle. Draw up tight to form flower shape and secure with a few sts.
With yellow yarn, embroider a few French knots in centre of flower.

Making up

Work in the ends neatly. Join the foot and back seams. Sew a flower to the centre of each strap. Sew a strap across the ankle of each bootee, securing them firmly on each side.

WAVE HEADBAND

Materials:
2 x balls of light worsted (DK/8-ply) alpaca/
   merino yarn – 1 x grey (A), 1 x dusky pink (B);
   50g/124yd/113m

Needles:
1 pair of 4mm (UK 8, US 6) knitting needles

Knitting note
When working from the chart, please note that the knit rows are the odd-numbered rows and the purl rows are the even-numbered rows. Remember to twist yarn every 3–4 sts to avoid large loops forming at the back of your work.

Instructions:

Using size 4mm (UK 8, US 6) knitting needles and yarn A, cast on 28 sts and ktbl to form a neat edge.

Join yarn B and continue by working the 10-row pattern from the chart below until work measures approximately 18in (46cm). This allows for some 'give' when placed around an adult's head.

Fasten off yarn B.

Knit 1 row in yarn A.

Cast off all sts.

Making up
With RS facing, join side seams together using mattress stitch. Weave in all loose ends.

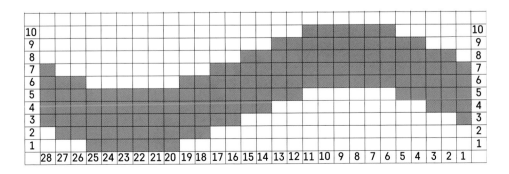

This alternative tree is made from sparkly white and silver fingering (4-ply) yarn, clear beads and a star button for a shimmering, snowy feel.

CHRISTMAS TREE

Materials:

1 ball of fingering (4-ply) yarn in green,
   50g/191yd/175m

Small amount of fingering (4-ply) yarn in red

Red beads

Small brass bell

Toy stuffing

Green sewing thread and sewing needle

Needles:

1 pair 2.75mm (UK 12, US 2) knitting
   needles

Size:

Approx. 3½in (9cm) tall

Instructions:

Tree (make two)

Using green yarn, cast on 3 sts.

K 1 row.

Work inc rows as follows:

k1, M1, k to last st, M1, k1 (5 sts).

K 1 row.

Rep these 2 rows three more times
(11 sts).

Cast off 3 sts at the beginning of the
next 2 rows (5 sts).

Next row: k1, M1, k to last st, M1, k1
(7 sts).

K 1 row.

Rep the last 2 rows four more times
(15 sts).

Cast off 4 sts at the beg of the next 2
rows (7 sts).

Next row: k1, M1, k to last st, M1, K1
(9 sts).

K 1 row.

Rep the last 2 rows five more times
(19 sts).

Cast off all sts.

Trunk

Using red yarn, cast on 10 sts and
work ¾in (2cm) in st st. Cast off.

Making up

Place the two tree shapes together
and sew them together, filling them
lightly with toy stuffing as you go.
Fold the trunk in half and attach it to
the base of the tree. Sew on beads
using a sewing needle and green
thread. Use the picture as a guide.
Attach the bell to the top of the tree.

These stylish mug hugs work well in a variety of colourways. Why not make a cosy pair for you and your loved one!

HEART MUG HUG

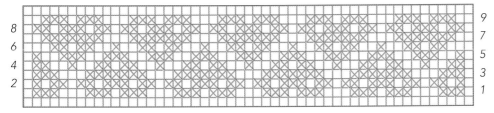

Materials:

1 ball of light worsted (DK/8-ply)
  yarn in dusty pink; 50g/137yd/125m

1 ball of light worsted (DK/8-ply) yarn in
  light blue

1 fancy matching button

Needles:

1 pair 4mm (UK 8, US 6)
  knitting needles

Size:

9¾ x 2¾in (25 x 7cm)

Instructions:

Using pink yarn, cast on 53 sts.
Work 4 rows in GS.
Join in blue yarn and knit 2 rows in
st st.
Join in pink yarn and work 9 rows in
Fair Isle pattern, working from the
chart. Read right-side rows from
right to left and strand yarn not in use
loosely across back of work. Pulling
the yarn too tightly will cause the
work to pucker.
When Fair Isle pattern is complete,
continue in blue yarn as follows:
Next row: purl.
Work 2 rows in st st.
Join in pink yarn and work 4 rows
in GS.
Cast off.

Button and buttonhole edges

With RS facing and using pink yarn,
pick up and knit 17 sts evenly along
one short edge.
Knit 1 row.
Working in GS, dec 1 st at each of
next and every alt row until 7 sts rem.
Cast off.
Work along other short edge in same
way until 11 sts rem.
Next row: to make the buttonhole,
k2tog, k3, yrn twice, k2tog, k2, k2tog.
Next row: knit, dropping the yrn of the
previous row and knitting into
the loops.
Continue to dec as before until 7
sts rem.
Cast off.

Making up

Work in all ends neatly and then sew
on the button to correspond with the
buttonhole at the other end.

Colour chart

FAIR ISLE
WRIST WARMERS

Materials:

3 balls of light worsted
(DK/8-ply) alpaca yarn – 1 x midnight
blue (A), 1 x mustard (B), 1 x parchment
(C); all 50g/131yd/120m

Needles:

1 pair of 4mm (UK 8, US 6)
knitting needles

Instructions:

Make two

Using 4mm (UK 8, US 6) needles and yarn A, cast on 40 sts, then ktbl to form a neat edge.

Rows 1–2: *k1, p1*, rep from * to * to end of row.

Row 3: Using yarn B, knit, inc 4 sts evenly across the row [44 sts].

NB: You are increasing on row 3 only.

Row 4: Using yarn B, purl.

Rows 5 and 7: k1B, *k1A, k3B*, rep from * to * to last 3 sts, k1A, k2B.

Row 6: *p1B, p1A*, rep from * to * end of row.

Rows 8–9: Starting with a purl row and using yarn B, st st.

Rows 10 and 12: *p1A, p3B*, rep from * to * to end of row.

Row 11: *k1A, k1B*, rep from * to * to end of row.

Rows 13–14: Using yarn B, st st.

Rows 15–16: Using yarn A, knit. Cut off yarn A.

Rows 17–18: Using yarn C, knit.

Rows 19–30: Work as rows 3–14, substituting yarn C for yarn A.

Rows 31–32: Using yarn C, knit.

Rows 33–34: Using yarn A, knit.

Rows 35–46: As rows 3–14. Cut off yarn B.

Row 47: Using yarn A, knit.

Row 48: Cast off all sts.

Making up

Join side seams using a tapestry needle and mattress stitch, 2¾in (7cm) from the wrist end (cast-on edge) and 2in (5cm) from the finger end. This will leave a gap for your thumb to go through.

Weave in all loose ends.

This is a very neat little scarf that will add fun and style to your wardrobe. For a different look change the central bow and add a large brooch. The scarf is easy to make once you have learnt how to cable.

RED ROOSTER SCARF

Materials:

2 balls of worsted/aran (10-ply) yarn in red;
100g/144yd/132m

Needles:

1 pair of 5.5mm (UK 5, US 9) knitting needles

Large-eyed tapestry needle

1 cable needle

Knitting note

c6b: slip next 3 sts on to a cable needle and hold at back of work, knit next 3 sts from left-hand needle, then knit sts from cable needle.

c6f: slip next 3 sts on to a cable needle and hold at front of work, then knit next sts from left-hand needle.

Instructions:

Initial rows

Rows 1–2: cast on 46 sts in red, ktbl on return row (i.e. row 2).

Double cable pattern

Row 1: p5, k36, p5.

Row 2: k5, p36, k5.

Row 3: p5, c6b, c6f. Repeat the twelve-stitch cable pattern twice more, p5.

Row 4: k5, p36, k5.

Rows 5 and 6: As rows 1 and 2.

Repeat the above six rows until work measures 32¼in (82cm), then repeat rows 1–4 once more. Cast off sts.

Making up

Measure 4¾in (12cm) from the cast-on/cast-off edges. Using a piece of yarn, gather the end of the scarf in, and wrap the wool several times around the middle tightly. Tie a knot and sew in any loose ends. Fan your knitting out to form your edge.

Making the bow

Cast on 16 sts in red.

Rows 1–16: Knit (garter stitch).

Cast off sts.

Fold knitting in half lengthways (short ends together). Using your tapestry needle and a piece of yarn do a series of running sts along the centre line and draw them in tightly to form the centre of the bow. Sew in your loose ends of yarn.

Completing the scarf

Cut six lengths of yarn, each measuring approximately 30in (76cm). Tie a knot at one end to hold the pieces together. Make a long plait using the strands in three pairs. Fold the completed plait in half and tie it around the centre of the bow.

To wear the scarf, wrap it around your neck crossing the two ends over each other. Hold the bow over the centre and tie the plaits together.

Instructions:

Body

Using cream yarn, cast on 14 sts, p 1 row.

Work inc rows as follows:

K1, (k1fb, k1, K1fb) to last st, k1. P 1 row (22 sts).

K1, (k1fb, k3, k1fb) to last st, k1. P 1 row (30 sts).

K1, (k1fb, k5, k1fb) to last st, k1. P 1 row (38 sts).

K1, (k1fb, k7, k1fb) to last st, k1. P 1 row (46 sts).

K1, (k1fb, K9, k1fb) to last st, k1. P 1 row (54 sts).

K1, (k1fb, k11, k1fb) to last st, k1. P 1 row (62 sts).

Work 2 rows in st st. Change to brown and work 4 rows in st st.

Materials:

Small amounts of fingering (4-ply) yarn in brown,
cream, red, dark grey and orange

Toy stuffing

Needles:

1 pair of 2.75mm (UK 12, US 2) DPN

Size:

Approx. 2⅜in (6cm) diameter body

ROCKING ROBIN

Work dec rows as follows:

K1, (k2tog, k11, ssk) to last st, k1. P 1 row (54 sts).

K1, (k2tog, k9, ssk) to last st, k1. P 1 row (46 sts).

K1, (k2tog, k7, ssk) to last st, k1. P 1 row (38 sts).

K1, (k2tog, k5, ssk) to last st, k1. P 1 row (30 sts).

K1, (k2tog, k3, ssk) to last st, k1. P 1 row (22 sts).

K1, (k2tog, k1, ssk) to last st, k1. P 1 row (14 sts).

Thread yarn through rem sts and fasten off.

Red breast

Using red yarn, cast on 14 sts and work 2 rows in st st.

Next row: k1, M1, k to last st, M1, k1. P 1 row.

Rep these 2 rows once more (18 sts).

Work 4 rows in st st.

Next row: k7, ssk, k2tog, k7 (16 sts). P 1 row.

Rep the last 2 rows, working 1 less st before and after dec shapings until 6 sts rem.

Work 4 rows in st st.

Next row: ssk, k2, k2tog.

Cast off rem 4 sts (WS).

Beak

Using orange yarn, cast on 5 sts and p 1 row.

Next row: ssk, k1, k2tog. Thread yarn through resulting 3 sts and sew seam.

Wings (make 2)

Using brown yarn, cast on 10 sts and work 2 rows in st st.

Next row: k1, M1, k to last st, M1, k1 (12 sts).

P 1 row. Rep these 2 rows once more (14 sts).

Work 2 rows in st st.

Next row: K1, ssk, K to last 3 sts, k2tog, k1 (12 sts).

P 1 row.

Rep the last 2 rows until 4 sts rem.

Next row: ssk, k2tog (2 sts).

K2tog and fasten off rem st.

Tail

Using brown yarn, cast on 7 sts and work in rib as follows:

Row 1: k1, p1 three times, K1.

Row 2: p1, K1 three times, p1.

Work a further 6 rows in k1, p1 rib.

Next row: k1, k2tog, p1, k2tog, k1 (5 sts).

Work 1 row as set in rib.

Next row: ssk, p1, k2tog (3 sts).

Work 1 row in rib and cast off rem sts.

Legs (make 2)

Using dark grey yarn, cast on 4 sts and work an i-cord (see page 84) 1⅝in (4cm) long. Thread yarn through sts and fasten.

Feet (make 2)

Each foot consists of three 'toes'. To make each toe, cast on 4 sts using dark grey yarn and work 4 rows of i-cord. Thread yarn through sts and fasten. Sew the three toes together.

Making up

Sew the side seam of the body and fill it with toy stuffing without distorting the shape. Sew the breast on to the front of the body with the RS showing, using the picture as a guide. Embroider the eyes using black yarn and attach the beak. Lightly press the wings and sew them on to the body at an angle. Sew the foot to the bottom of the leg. Repeat for the second leg and sew the legs on to the body.

A rose makes the perfect corsage on a coat, jacket or sweater. A cluster of roses would make a pretty decoration for a hat or bag. Pink yarn also makes a lovely rose – but roses come in all colours, so choose your favourite.

ROSE CORSAGE

Materials:
Small amount of light worsted (DK/8-ply) wool
    yarn in red

Needles:
Pair of 3mm (UK 11, US 2) knitting needles
Tapestry needle

Size:
3¹⁄₈in (8cm) across

Instructions:

Petal (make 6)

With red yarn, cast on 2 sts.

Row 1: inc in each st (4 sts).

Row 2: inc 1, k to end.

Row 3: inc 1, p to last st, k1.

Rep rows 2 and 3 until there are 10 sts.

Knit 8 rows.

Next row: k2tog, k6, k2tog (8 sts).

Next row: k2tog, p4, k2tog.

Next row: k2tog, k2, K2tog.

Next row: k2tog twice.

Next row: k2tog.

Fasten off.

Flower centre

With red yarn, cast on 108 sts.

Row 1: k all sts tbl.

Row 2: p2tog to end of row (54 sts).

Row 3: k.

Row 4: (p2tog, p4) to end of row (45 sts).

Row 5: k.

Row 6: (p2tog, p3) to end of row (36 sts).

Row 7: k.

Row 8: p2tog to end of row (18 sts).

Row 9: k.

Row 10: p2tog to end of row (9 sts).

Break yarn and thread through rem sts.

Making up

Curl the centre into a spiral and pull up the tail of yarn to gather the base, then secure it with a few stitches.

Stitch petals one at a time around the centre, with the cast-off edge of each petal at the base of the flower.

JEWELLERY KNOW-HOW

There are a number of basic materials and tools that are common to many different types of jewellery making.

Materials

Chain This can be purchased in all kinds of sizes, shapes and colours.

Jump ring This is a metal loop with a cut in it and is the most common connector for jewellery making.

Head pins and eye pins These help to link beads and buttons on to chain.

Waxed nylon cord, **beading thread**, **copper wire**, **beading elastic**, **leather thong**, **ribbon** and **embroidery thread** are all alternatives to **chain**.

Beads Various types are used in jewellery making: metal, freshwater pearl, spacer beads, glass, flat-back cabochons, crystal, seed beads and crimp beads.

Pewter and **leather** These are used in specialist types of jewellery making.

Findings These include earring hooks, cord end crimps, lobster clasps, stud earrings and butterflies, ring and bar clasps, hairslides, split rings and bolt rings.

Tools

Flat-nosed pliers These help to flatten crimp beads, hold wires in position and open and close jump rings.

Round-nosed pliers These help to create smooth loops of wire, and to finish off wire-wrapped loops. **Half round-nosed pliers** are very useful for curving wire and attaching jewellery findings.

Cutting pliers These are mostly used for cutting wire, as they leave the cut edge smooth and even.

Scissors These are for cutting cord or elastic.

Leather scissors These are special ones for leather jewellery making, as they are much stronger than normal scissors.

Ruler This helps you to measure and cut lengths of wire and cord.

Wire cutters Use these to cut jewellery or craft wire.

Split-eye or beading needle This type of needle is ideal for stringing lots of beads as it has a very large eye.

Beading mat This helps to stop materials rolling on to the floor.

Ring mandrel This tool has markings on it to indicate different ring sizes. It will help ensure that your ring starts out, and stays, the size you want it to be when finished. It will also ensure that the ring stays round, so it will be comfortable to wear.

Thread zapper or clear contact glue A thread zapper heats and fuses thread so that you do not need to use glue. Alternatively, you may prefer to use **liquid jewellery glue** to join threads. **Leather glue** will be needed to stick leather together.

File This is used to file off any sharp ends that might be present on the jewellery wire.

Cocktail sticks and **tweezers** These are useful for positioning beads and other decorative items before sticking them down.

Kebab sticks These can be useful for applying small amounts of glue to jewellery items, and **wax sticks** (simply a kebab stick with a small amount of wax on the end) are good for picking up flat-back crystals and other beads and transferring them into place.

For the Pewter Heart Necklace:

You will need a basic pewter kit to make the pendant on page 146:

Tracer tool A small ball tip or rounded tip similar to a knitting needle; used for 'drawing' the design on to the face of the pewter.

Cardboard The cardboard from the back of the tracing paper pad will work well.

Thick tracing paper (90gsm) and **HB pencil**

Masking tape This is used to hold the pewter in place.

Glue Any glue compatible with both metal and the surface onto which you are affixing it. Silicon-based glue is good for pewter, and clear epoxy glue is great to adhere crystals, beads and semi-precious stone to the pewter design.

You will also need these basic polishing materials:

Hard non-textured surface	Turpentine
Cotton wool	Baby powder
Rubber or latex gloves	Patina
Tissues	Household metal polish

Instructions for polishing:

1 Place the pewter with its design side up on to the hard surface. Clean the front of the pewter, first with a piece of cotton wool dipped into the baby powder. Note: the patina will not take if the pewter is not clean.

2 Wearing the gloves, absorb a little patina on to a small piece of cotton wool and apply evenly over the piece of pewter. It will blacken very quickly; once black, stop applying patina.

3 Rinse the pewter under the tap and pat dry with a tissue.

4 Absorb a little metal polish on to a piece of cotton wool and rub it over the face of the pewter. Buff off gently with a clean piece of cotton wool.

NB: rubbing too hard or buffing dry polish will remove the top layer of the pewter, making it duller.

133

For the Butterfly Friendship Bracelet:

The technique below is used to make the square knots in the butterfly friendship bracelet on page 140.

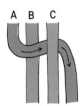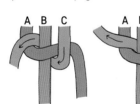

1 Pass cord A over B and under C.

2 Pass cord C under B and over A.

3 Pull cord A and cord C tight to create half the square knot.

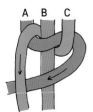

4 Pass cord A over B and under C.

5 Pass cord C over A, under B and over A. Pull the cords tight to complete the square knot.

For the Beaded Felt Hairslide:

The pretty hairslide on page 156 uses the simple technique (right) of rolling the felt around a wooden skewer or cocktail stick. The bead is then fastened together with glue or thread, and decorated with coloured thread, tiny beads and other embellishments. The hole in the centre of the bead can be used to thread it onto cord, depending on what you are making.

SEA BRIDE BRACELET

Materials:

11 green handmade
   glass beads

11 silver eye pins

1 decorative ring and bar clasp

2 silver jump rings

Tools:

Flat-nosed pliers

Half round-nosed pliers

Wire cutters

Instructions:

1 Thread a glass bead on to an eye pin. Using flat-nosed pliers bend the wire to a right angle and then cut, leaving ⅜in (1cm) of wire above the bead.

2 Using the round-nosed pliers bend the wire into a loop. Just before closing the loop fully, thread on another eye pin, then repeat this process ten more times.

3 Finally, attach a jump ring to the last eye pin, then attach the ring and bar clasp to each end of the linked beads.

This bracelet was made using the same techniques with metal beads in place of the glass ones.

PRECIOUS STONE NECKLACE

Materials:

Pendant with central hole

2 medium metal beads

39½in (1m) suede ribbon

2 flat leather crimps

4 crimp beads

Lobster clasp

Tools:

Round-nosed pliers

Flat-nosed pliers

Scissors

Instructions:

1 Place the two ends of suede together and pass the loop through the central hole of the pendant. Pass the two ends of suede through the loop and pull up, securing the suede on to the pendant.

2 Thread on a crimp bead at the base of each length of suede just above the pendant. Secure them using flat-nosed pliers.

3 Thread a metal bead on to each length of suede and add another crimp bead above each bead.

4 Finish by attaching the flat leather crimps and lobster clasp after sizing the necklace to fit.

This natural-looking necklace has knots instead of crimp beads around the copper-coloured beads.

Materials:

13¾in (35cm) of 1.5mm silver-plated copper wire

8 ft 11½in (2.73m) of 0.5mm silver-plated copper wire

Four 5mm silver-plated spacer beads

3 metal daisy shank buttons

Tools:

Flat-nosed pliers

Round-nosed pliers

Wire cutters

Liquid jewellery glue

File

Beading mat

Ruler

DAISY BUTTON BANGLE

Instructions:

1 Cut the 1.5mm wire to length and file the ends. This will become the core of the bracelet.

2 Cut a 24in (61cm) length of the 0.5mm wire. Hold both wires ¾in (2cm) from the ends. Wrap the thinner wire around the core, keeping it very tight and not overlapping it.

3 Once all the thin wire is wrapped around the core, cut any stray ends flush with the core and file any sharp ends. Bend in the thin wire ends so they sit close to the core using the flat-nosed pliers.

4 Repeat steps 2 and 3 twice more.

5 You should now have approximately 5⅞in (15cm) of wire wrapped centrally on the core. Now thread three daisy shank buttons on to the centre of the wire-wrapped core.

6 Secure the buttons by cutting a 4in (10cm) length of 0.5mm wire and wrapping it around the core in a criss-cross fashion surrounding the shank. Make sure the buttons are facing the same way.

7 Place two spacer beads on one end of the remaining core and then wrap the next ¾in (2cm) of core, with 11¾in (30cm) of the thinner wire. Do not wrap right to the end of the core. Do this on both ends.

8 Use round-nosed pliers to curl the ends of the bangle in tightly to create opposite facing spirals. Try to make sure the wrapped wire stays close to the beads and doesn't move to the end of the core wire.

9 Now bend the bangle into the shape of your wrist as smoothly as you can.

10 Dab a small amount of jewellery glue on to the underside of your buttons to secure firmly in place. Leave to dry.

If you prefer something steeped in ancient history, then try using bronze wire with a metal Celtic style button.

Use fuchsia pink butterfly beads, coin beads and heart beads alternating with 10mm silver beads to create a feminine look for summer.

BUTTERLY FRIENDSHIP BRACELET

Materials:

- 20in (50cm) of black 1mm waxed nylon cord
- 8 ceramic butterfly beads in red, green, purple and blue

Tools:

- Scissors
- Thread zapper or jewellery glue

Instructions:

1 Cut a length of cord 14in (35cm) long and tie a knot 3¼in (8cm) from one end.

2 Thread your first bead on to the cord from the long end and slide it up to the knot. Tie a knot after the bead to hold it in place.

3 Continue to thread on your beads and knot after each one until all the beads are used.

4 Cross the two cord ends and, using the remaining piece of cord, complete five square knots (see page 133) over the two strands to form a sliding knot.

5 Tie a simple knot in each of the cord ends.

6 Trim all the ends and finish using either the thread zapper or clear glue.

Tip

If you are using beads with a slightly larger hole, use a double strand of cord to create a larger knot between the beads.

A diamante encrusted key hangs from this keyhole variation.

STEAMPUNK BUTTERFLY RING

Materials:
Openwork metal ring base
2 butterfly charms
3 pearl flat-back cabochons
Jewellery adhesive

Tools:
Flat-nosed pliers
Cocktail stick
Tweezers

Instructions:

1 Carefully bend the larger butterfly to fit the shape of the ring base using the pliers. Glue to the centre of the ring base.

2 Use tweezers to position the smaller butterfly to the centre of the larger butterfly and glue it in place.

3 Glue the pearl cabochons to the top and sides of the butterfly using a cocktail stick to help with positioning.

GRECIAN PEARLS TIARA

Materials:

16 potato-shaped
  freshwater pearls

Ten 4mm pale gold
  crystal beads

Gold-plated tiara band

39½in (100cm) length of
  0.4mm gold-plated wire

Tools:

Flat-nosed pliers

Side-cutter pliers

Instructions:

1 First cut a 39½in (100cm) length
of wire and bend one end so that the
beads do not slide off. Thread on a
crystal, followed by two pearls and
then a crystal. Repeat until all the
beads are on the wire.

2 To secure the beads to the band,
wrap the longer, bare end of the
wire around the band, passing it
between the beads to hold them
tightly in place.

3 Secure the excess wire at each
end by wrapping it tightly around the
band and flattening it using the flat-
nosed pliers.

*This subtle tiara can be enhanced
with lots of single pearl and crystal
pins, making a simple but effective
hair decoration.*

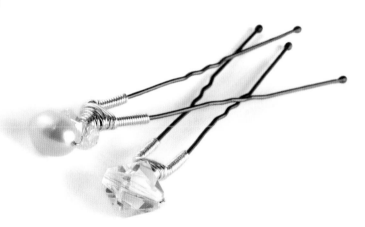

PEWTER HEART NECKLACE

Materials:

Pink, square beads and pink seed beads

Small wooden heart painted pink

Beading thread for stringing beads

Pink, flat-back crystals

Small eye hook

Jump ring

Pewter

Tools:

Basic pewter kit: tracer tool, cardboard, 90 gsm tracing paper (a similar thickness to regular printer paper), an HB pencil, masking tape and any glue compatible with both metal and wood

Polishing materials (see page 133)

2 pairs of flat-nosed pliers

Small scissors

Wax stick and kebab stick

Instructions:

1 Make up the beaded necklace by threading the beads on to the beading thread, alternating one seed bead and one square bead. A suitable, ready-made necklace is also an option.

2 Trace the heart design (below right) on to the tracing paper using the HB pencil. Place the pewter on to the cardboard; secure it in place with masking tape. Place the traced design on to the pewter and secure it with tape.

3 Trace the design on to the pewter using the tracer tool.

4 Complete the polishing process.

5 Cut out the heart design, using the small pair of scissors, and glue it in place on to the pink wooden heart.

6 Screw the small eye hook into the top of the wooden heart.

7 Use the flat-nose pliers to open the jump ring, hook the eye hook and necklace on to the jump ring, and then close the jump ring using the pliers.

8 Dip the kebab stick into the glue and place a small dab of glue on to the pewter where the crystals will be placed. Pick up the individual crystals with the tip of the wax stick and place each crystal on to the glue. Allow the glue to dry thoroughly.

This red and gold version of the charm makes a really dazzling decoration for a plain bag.

BUBBLE GUM CHARM

Materials:

3 large beaded beads

6 small faux pearls

2 medium faux pearls

Large silver-coloured craft chain

6 headpins

9 silver-coloured jump rings

Silver-coloured keyring fob

Tools:

Cutting pliers

Round-nosed pliers

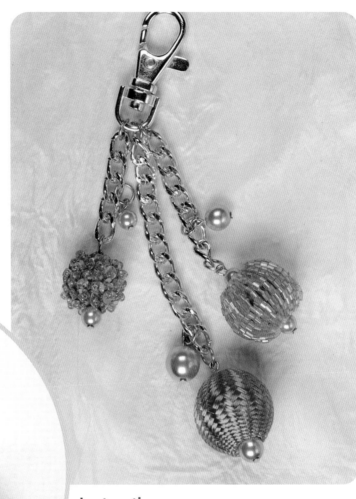

Instructions:

1 Wire the large beaded beads on to headpins, placing a small pearl bead at the top and bottom of each bead, and creating a loop at the top of each set of beads. Here, the smaller beaded bead did not need a pearl at the top; just use your own judgment when choosing beads.

2 Cut three pieces of craft chain of varying lengths and attach them to the keyring fob with jump rings.

3 Attach the three beaded beads to the base of each chain using jump rings, placing the largest bead on to the longest length of chain.

4 Wire the remaining pearls on to headpins and attach them to the chain as you wish.

For a stronger, bolder look, replace the round metal beads with wooden rectangular beads.

CELTIC BRACELET

Materials:

- 12in (30cm) of beading elastic
- Fifteen 8mm metal round beads
- 1 silver jump ring
- 1 silver decorative metal rectangular bead
- 1 metal cross pendant

Tools:

- Flat-nosed pliers
- Round-nosed pliers
- Scissors
- Jewellery glue

Instructions:

1 Thread the 12in (30cm) length of beading elastic with fifteen round metal beads, and then a silver rectangular bead.

2 Tie the two ends of the elastic together with a reef knot, pulling the beads up tightly as you tie. Dot the knot with glue and leave to dry.

3 When the glue is dry, trim the ends of the elastic and then pull the knot inside the silver rectangular metal bead.

4 Attach the metal cross to the side of the rectangular bead with a jump ring.

CALLA LILY EARRINGS

Instructions:

1 Draw a petal shape onto a piece of card measuring 1¼ x 1½in (3 x 4cm). Cut this out to use as a template. Draw around the template onto the leather and cut out two petal shapes.

2 Cut two lengths of wire with wire cutters, one measuring 2¼in (6cm) long and the other measuring 2in (5cm).

3 Thread a bead onto each of the lengths of wire and coil the end of the wire twice with the round-nosed pliers.

4 Place the two pieces of wire on top of a leather petal shape with the pointed end of the petal at the top. Position the wires so that the beads are slightly lower than the base of the petal and so that the top of the wires are aligned.

5 Apply a little glue to the top of the petal and roll the ends together to form the calla lily shape. Form a loop with the two excess pieces of wire and wrap the excess wire around the base of the loop and around the top of the leather. Attach an earwire to the loop.

6 Repeat the process for the second earring.

This ring gives off a timeless elegance with clusters of dazzling crystals on a band of yet more glistening crystals! Alternatively, use grey pearls for a more subtle look (see opposite).

STATEMENT RING

Instructions:

1 Use the wire cutters to cut the ball end head pins to about ¾in (2cm) – enough to create two coil loops above a 6mm crystal bead.

2 Thread a 6mm faceted crystal onto a ball end head pin and make a coil loop with the round-nose pliers. Repeat with all the 6mm crystals (about 10).

3 Thread about ¾–1¼in (2–3cm) of cord through the split-eye needle, then pass it through about 14–16 of the 3mm crystals (the number of crystal rondelles is determined by the size of ring required).

4 Add the 6mm crystals by threading them through the coil loops.

5 Remove the needle and tie the two ends of the cord together using a double surgeon's knot (see below).

6 Pull the beads aside to expose the knot. Tug gently until the knot catches.

7 Coat the knot with clear nail polish to seal and secure.

8 Allow the nail polish to dry, then snip the excess cord. Pull the beads round to conceal the knot.

Materials:

Approx. 14–16 3mm faceted round crystal AB (aurora borealis finish)

10 6mm faceted round crystal AB

10 ball end head pins

Stretchy cord

Clear nail polish

Tools:

Scissors

Wire cutters

Round-nose pliers

Split-eye needle

How to make a double surgeon's knot

1 Cross the left end of the cord over the right end, and bring it round twice, then pull.

2 Cross the right end of the cord over the left end of the cord and bring it round twice, then pull.

3 Now pull all four strands that are coming out of the knot tightly until it catches (pull the two on the left to the left, and the two on the right to the right).

4 Glue the knot to seal and secure it.

1

2

3

4

BEADED FELT HAIRSLIDE

Materials:

2 rust-coloured felt pieces,
   3¼ x 4¼in (8 x 11cm)

Selection of black seed beads

Rust-coloured
   embroidery thread

Copper-coloured sparkly
   embroidery thread

Beading thread

Two 2⅜in (6cm) hairslides

Tools:

Scissors

Beading needle

Needle

Instructions:

1 Bind the felt pieces into long beads using embroidery thread, following the simple rolling technique shown on page 133.

2 Bind the open ends of the beads with blanket stitch and decorate them with sparkly thread.

3 Attach seed beads to the top surface of each felt bead, making sure that the back of each bead remains free of decoration.

4 Stitch each felt bead securely on to a hairslide, using the holes provided in the back of each slide.

You could use these hairslides to complement a special dress. Simply match the colour to your chosen outfit.

CROCHET KNOW-HOW

US and UK crochet terminology

The names for basic crochet stitches differ in the UK and the US. In all patterns, US terms are given first (see Abbreviations opposite), followed by the UK terms in brackets – for example, US single crochet is written as sc (*UKdc*), and US double crochet as dc (*UKtr*).

Yarn

The crochet projects here use a range of different yarns. See Knitting know-how (pages 82–85) for more information on types of yarn.

Gauge (tension)

Many of the projects have been given an approximate completed size, but not a specific gauge (tension). It is not essential to achieve any particular gauge on items that are accessories, so if they turn out a bit bigger or smaller it will not make much difference. However, the finished guide should provide a basic idea of what size your completed project should be if you use yarn of a similar weight. The only projects that have been given a gauge guide throughout are the beanies, and here it is useful to work a gauge sample so that you can be sure that your project will be the size you want.

Crochet hooks

It is essential to work with a hook that is easy on your hands. Crochet hooks are made from aluminium, steel, plastic, bamboo and wood. It is best to experiment with different types to find one that suits you and offers comfort and control.

Other tools and materials

You will need various items such as purse clasps, scraps of fabric for linings, scraps of ribbon, a good pair of scissors for cutting fabric and yarn ends, a tapestry needle for weaving in loose ends and sewing on motifs, and a standard sewing needle and thread.

For some projects it may also be useful to have some iron-on medium-weight interfacing, although this is optional. You will also need beads, faux pearls, ear wires, jump rings and chain for some of the projects; these items are all listed with the patterns.

Blocking

The purpose of blocking is to finish off a piece of crochet, make it look regular and professional, and 'set' the stitches. Flat pieces of crochet often benefit from blocking, especially if they are liable to curl at the edges. All you need is a large piece of foam about 1in (2.5cm) thick, a clean towel, a can of spray fabric stiffener (starch), or spray bottle filled with warm water, and some pins.

1 Lay the towel over the piece of foam.

2 Place your piece of crochet in the middle of the towel and spray it with the fabric stiffener or warm water so it is saturated.

3 Now pin out your crochet carefully to the shape you want. You may need to use a ruler if you want a shape of exact dimensions.

4 Leave it to dry, making sure it remains undisturbed.

5 Once it is completely dry, unpin your crochet and it will be a nice, flat regular shape.

Crochet Abbreviations

The abbreviations listed below are the most frequently used terms in the book. Any special abbreviations in a crochet pattern are explained on the relevant project page.

US	UK
sl st (slip stitch)	sl st (slip stitch)
ch st (chain stitch)	ch st (chain stitch)
ch sp (chain space)	ch sp (chain space)
sc (single crochet)	dc (double crochet)
hdc (half double crochet)	htr (half treble crochet)
dc (double crochet)	tr (treble crochet)
tr (treble crochet)	dtr (double treble crochet)
dtr (double treble crochet)	trtr (triple treble crochet)
skip	miss
yrh (yarn round hook)	yrh (yarn round hook)
beg (beginning)	beg (beginning)
rep (repeat)	rep (repeat)
sp/s (space(s))	sp/s (space(s))

Crochet stitch symbols

The beanie hats in this section use crochet charts in which you will see the symbols listed below. However, crochet symbols are not universal, so be sure to consult the key that comes with your pattern when using other books.

Key for crochet pattern diagrams

o = 1 ch

• = 1 sl st

× = 1 sc (UKdc)

= 1 hdc (UKhtr)

= 1 dc (UKtr)

= 1 tr (UKdtr)

= dc2tog, dc3tog or dc4tog (UKtr2tog, tr3tog, tr4tog)

= dc2tog or dc3tog (UKtr2tog, tr3tog)

= dc4tog or dc6tog (UKtr4tog, tr6tog)

= 3 or 4 dc (UKtr) stitches worked in the same stitch

= 5 or 6 dc (UKtr) stitches worked in the same stitch

= 2, 3 or 4 incomplete dc (UKtr) stitches worked in the same stitch

Tip
If the symbols are joined together at the bottom, then the stitches are crocheted in the same stitch. If the symbols are joined together at the top, then the stitches are drawn through together.

159

GLITTERY BEANIE

Materials:

2 balls of Schachenmayr SMC Alpaca or similar light worsted (DK/8-ply) yarn camel; 50g/109yd/100m

1 ball of Anchor Artiste Metallic Fine crochet thread in gold, or similar; 25g/273yd/250m

Tools:

5mm (US H/8, UK 6) and 6mm (US J/10, UK 4) crochet hooks

Size:

Head circumference 21¼–23in (54–58cm)

Gauge (tension) sample

16 sts and 9 rounds in the basic pattern using the 6mm (US J/10, UK 4) crochet hook = 4 x 4in (10 x 10cm). Change your hook if necessary to obtain the correct gauge (tension).

Basic pattern

Crochet following the crochet pattern using a 6mm (US J/10, UK 4) hook and working with both yarns held double (one yarn in camel, one yarn in gold). Work the 1st–6th rounds once, then continue repeating the crochet pattern for the 5th and 6th rounds. Every round ends with 1 sl st into the 3rd or 1st ch from the start of the round; see the crochet pattern below.

Instructions:

Start the beanie at the crown and work down to the bottom edge in the basic pattern following the chart (right).

Using the 2 yarns together and the 6mm (US J/10, UK 4) hook, begin with 4 ch and join into a ring with a sl st.

Round 1: Begin with 5 ch (1st 3 ch represent the 1st dc [UKtr]). Then work * 1dc (UKtr), 2 ch * , rep from * to * 6 times and join with a sl st to the 3rd ch from the start of the round.

Rounds 2–6: Follow the chart, working the dc (UKtr) or sc (UKdc) into the gaps under the ch sts of the previous round. Start every round with the appropriate number of ch as shown: 3 ch replaces the 1st dc (UKtr); 1 ch replaces the 1st sc (UKdc). The numbers show the round transitions.

Round 7 onwards: Rep rounds 5–6 until the piece measure 10½in (27cm) from the foundation ch with a 6th pattern round.

Hat band

Change to the 5mm (US H/8, UK 6) hook and 2 strands of the gold yarn, and work 1 sc (UKdc) into each dc (UKtr) and each ch of the previous round. Work 3 more rounds, working sc (UKdc) into each st around. Finish the final round with a sl st into the 1st st of the round. Fasten off all yarn ends neatly.

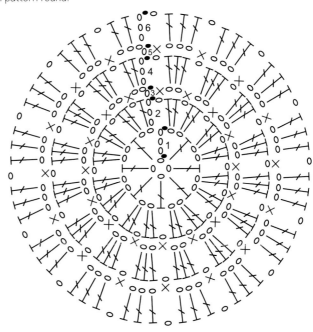

CHRISTMAS STOCKING

Materials:

- 1 ball of No. 3 crochet cotton in red and a small amount in white; 100g/306yd/280m
- 4 snowflake buttons (8 if you wish to embellish both sides)
- Silver ribbon bow
- 20in (0.5m) of narrow silver ribbon
- Sewing thread to match the buttons and ribbon

Tools:

- 2mm (US B/1, UK 14) crochet hook
- Sewing needle

Size:

Approx. 4in (10cm) high

Instructions:

Using white crochet cotton, make 29 ch.

Row 1: 1 sc (UKdc) into 2nd ch from hook, 1 sc (UKdc) into each ch to end; turn (28 sts).

Rows 2–3: work 1 sc (UKdc) into each sc (UKdc) to end.

Row 4: join in red. *Insert hook into first sc (UKdc) and pull yarn through, then insert hook into corresponding sc (UKdc) 2 rows below, draw up loop and work as normal sc (UKdc),* repeat to end.

Row 5: using red, work 1 row in sc (UKdc).

Row 6: using white, work 1 row in sc (UKdc).

Row 7: using white, repeat row 4.

Row 8: using white, work 1 row in sc (UKdc).

Rows 9–20: using red, work each st in sc (UKdc).

Now create the top of the foot:

Row 1: work in sc (UKdc) across 18 sts, turn.

Row 2: work in sc (UKdc) across 8 sts, turn.

Rows 3–10: work in sc (UKdc) on these 8 sts. Fasten off yarn.

Foot

Rejoin yarn and work 10 sc (UKdc) along the right side of the top of the foot, 8 sc (UKdc) across the toe, and 10 sc (UKdc) down the left side of top of the foot then finally work across the remaining 10 sc (UKdc) of the foot (48 sts), turn.

Rows 1–6: work in sc (UKdc) across all sts.

Row 7: sc (UKdc) 2 tog, sc (UKdc) 20, sc (UKdc) 2 tog twice, sc (UKdc) 20, sc (UKdc) 2 tog.

Row 8: sc (UKdc) 2 tog, sc (UKdc) 18, sc (UKdc) 2 tog twice, sc (UKdc) 18, sc (UKdc) 2 tog.

Row 9: sc (UKdc) 2 tog, sc (UKdc) 16, sc (UKdc) 2 tog twice, sc (UKdc) 16, sc (UKdc) 2 tog.

Row 10: sc (UKdc) 2 tog, sc (UKdc) 14, sc (UKdc) 2 tog twice, sc (UKdc) 14, sc (UKdc) 2 tog.

Row 11: sc (UKdc) 2 tog, work in sc (UKdc) to last 2 sts, sc (UKdc) 2 tog; fasten off.

Making up

Weave in the loose yarn ends and sew the foot and back seam of the stocking. Attach the snowflake buttons and the ribbon bow, using the photograph as a guide. Fold the silver ribbon in half to make a hanging loop, trimming it to the required length, and attach it to the stocking.

TEDDY BEAR

Materials

- Approx. half a ball of No. 5 crochet cotton or a fine 4-ply yarn; 50g/191yd/175m
- Small amount of toy stuffing

Tools:

- 2.5mm (US B1, UK 13) crochet hook
- Tapestry needle

Size:

- Approx. 4¼in (11cm) in height when sitting

Crochet note

When working the pieces, it is a good idea to mark the beginning of each round to avoid losing or even gaining stitches. Fill each part with small amounts of toy stuffing as you work; avoid over-filling.

Gauge (tension)

5 sc (*UKdc*) measure 1in (2.5cm) in width using the stated hook, though gauge (tension) is not critical when making these bears if you are prepared to accept a small variation in size.

Instructions:

Head

Row 1: with the appropriate colour yarn, make 2 ch, 6 sc (*UKdc*) in 2nd ch from hook, join in a circle with a sl st.

Row 2: 1 ch, 2 sc (*UKdc*) in each sc (*UKdc*) all round, join with a sl st (12 sts).

Rows 3–5: work in sc (*UKdc*).

Join the contrasting yarn, if stated in the instructions, and proceed as follows:

Row 6: *1 sc (*UKdc*) in next sc (*UKdc*), 2 sc (*UKdc*) in next sc (*UKdc*)*, rep from * to * all round.

Rows 7 and 8: work in sc (*UKdc*).

Row 9: inc 6 sc (*UKdc*) evenly in row.

Rows 10–15: work in sc (*UKdc*).

Row 16: dec 6 sc (*UKdc*) evenly in row.

Row 17: work in sc (*UKdc*).

Row 18: dec 6 sc (*UKdc*) evenly in row.

Row 19: work in sc (*UKdc*).

Row 20: dec 4 sc (*UKdc*) evenly in row.

Break yarn and run through last row. Draw up and fasten off.

Body

Row 1: with the appropriate colour yarn, make 2 ch, work 6 sc (*UKdc*) in 2nd ch from hook, join with a sl st to form a tight circle.

Subsequent rows are all joined with a sl st unless otherwise stated.

Row 2: 2 sc (*UKdc*) in each dc (*UKdc*) all round, join as before (12 sts).

Row 3: *1 sc (*UKdc*) in next st, 2 sc (*UKdc*) in next sc (*UKdc*)*, rep from * to * all round (18 sts).

Row 4: *1 sc (*UKdc*) in each of next 2 sc (*UKdc*), 2 sc (*UKdc*) in next sc (*UKdc*)*, rep from * to * all round (24 sts).

Row 5: *1 sc (*UKdc*) in each of next 3 sc (*UKdc*), 2 sc (*UKdc*) in next sc (*UKdc*)*, rep from * to * all round (30 sts).

Rows 6–18: sc (*UKdc*).

Row 19: dec 6 sts evenly all round (24 sts).

Row 20: sc (*UKdc*).

Rep rows 19 and 20 until 6 sc (*UKdc*) rem.

Finish stuffing the body, break yarn and run the thread through the last row. Draw up and fasten off.

Arms (make 2)

Row 1: with the appropriate colour yarn, make 2 ch, 7 sc (*UKdc*) in 2nd ch from hook, join in a tight circle with a sl st.

Row 2: 2 sc (*UKdc*) in each st, 14 sc (*UKdc*), join with a sl st.

Rows 3–14: sc (*UKdc*).

Row 15: *sc (*UKdc*) 2 tog, 1 sc (*UKdc*) in next sc (*UKdc*)*, rep from * to * all round.

Row 16: sc (*UKdc*) all round. Break yarn.

Complete the stuffing, pushing a little extra into the base of the arm to form the paw. Pull up to close. This is the top of the arm.

Legs (make 2)

The foot is shaped, so push a little extra stuffing into that area as you work.

Row 1: with the appropriate colour yarn, make 2 ch, 7 sc (*UKdc*) in 2nd ch from hook, join in a tight circle with a sl st.

Row 2: 2 sc (*UKdc*) in each st, 14 sc (*UKdc*), join with a sl st.

Row 3: *1 sc (*UKdc*), 2 sc (*UKdc*) in next st*, rep from * to *, working 1 sc (*UKdc*) in last st (20 sts).

Rows 4–6: sc (*UKdc*) all round.

Row 7: 7 sc (*UKdc*), [sc (*UKdc*) 2 tog] 3 times, 7 sc (*UKdc*).

Rows 8–17: sc (*UKdc*) all round.

Row 18: dec 3 sts evenly all round.

Row 19: sc (*UKdc*) all round.

Row 20: dec 3 sts evenly all round.

Break yarn, draw yarn through last row of sc (*UKdc*), draw up and fasten off.

Ears (make 2)

Row 1: with the appropriate colour yarn, make 2 ch, 7 sc (*UKdc*) in 2nd ch from hook, join into a circle.

Row 2: 2 sc (*UKdc*) in each sc (*UKdc*) all round.

Row 3: sc (*UKdc*) all round. Fasten off.

Making up

Work in all the loose ends. Sew the head firmly to the body. You can position the head at different angles to give the bear more character. Pin the ears on each side of the head, and when you are happy with their position, sew them on firmly. Embroider the nose and eyes on to the head of the bear, then stitch a straight line from the centre of the nose to the chin, and a thin line above the eyes to make the eyebrows. Sew the arms in position on either side of the bear's shoulders. Attach the legs, one on each side, in a sitting position. Make sure they are level so that your bear sits down properly.

ORANGE BLOSSOM

Materials:

Small amounts of No. 3 crochet cotton in yellow
and white

Selection of small orange beads

Orange sewing thread

Tools:

2.5mm (US B1, UK 13) crochet hook

Sewing needle

Tapestry needle

Instructions:

Using yellow crochet cotton, make 4 ch, join with a sl st
into a ring.

Round 1: 1 ch, 5 sc (*UKdc*) into ring, ss into 1 ch.

Round 2: 2 ch, 1 dc (*UKtr*) into each sc (*UKdc*), ss to join,
tie off the end.

Rejoin white crochet cotton at base of work, work into sc
(*UKdc*) strand.

Round 3: *6 ch, miss 1 ch, 1 sc (*UKdc*) into next ch, 1 hdc
(*UKhtr*) into next ch, 1 dc (*UKtr*) into next ch, 1 tr (*UKdtr*)
into next ch, 1 dtr (*UKttr*) into next ch, ss into next st of
first round*, repeat from * to * 4 more times, making 5
petals in total. End in same st as join.

Tie off and sew in the ends.

Join the sewing thread to the reverse of the flower and
push the needle up through the space between the yellow
centre and the white ridge surrounding it. Thread on a
bead and take the thread back through to the back of
the work. Repeat, sewing on beads all around the yellow
flower centre.

*These pretty little flowers look great on accessories
around the home – try them on hanging hearts,
napkin rings, jewellery boxes and even your
Christmas tree to add that personal touch.*

CHRISTMAS STAR

Instructions:

Using white crochet cotton, make 6 ch then join with a sl st into a ring.
Round 1: 1 ch, work 12 sc (UKdc) into the ring then join with sl st to first ch.
Round 2: 5 ch, miss 1 sc (UKdc), sc (UKdc) into next sc (UKdc), all around, join to 1st of 5 ch at beg of round (six 5 ch loops).
Round 3: sl st into first 5 ch loop, 2 ch, work 5 dc (UKtr) into same loop, 1 sc (UKdc) in next sc (UKdc). *6 dc (UKtr) into 5 ch loop, 1 sc (UKdc) into next sc (UKdc),* repeat from * to * 4 times more and then join with a sl st to beg of round.
Round 4: sl st to 2nd dc (UKtr), 2 ch, 1 dc (UKtr) into same dc (UKtr), 2 dc (UKtr) into each of next 3 dc (UKtr), 1 sc (UKdc) into next sc (UKdc), *miss next dc (UKtr), 2 dc (UKtr) into each of next 4 dc (UKtr), miss 1 dc (UKtr), 1 sc (UKdc) into sc (UKdc),* repeat from * to * 4 times more and then join with a sl st to beg of round. Break off white.

Round 5: join in metallic yarn to same place as sl st and proceed as follows. Work *1 sc (UKdc) into each of the next 4 dc (UKtr), **4 ch, sl st into 3rd ch from hook (1 picot formed),** repeat from ** to ** twice more, 1 sc (UKdc) into each of the next 4 dc (UKtr), 1 sc (UKdc) into sc (UKdc) of row 4, thus pulling up a long loop,* repeat from * to * 5 times more and then join with a sl st to beg of round. Fasten off.

Making up

Using white thread, stitch the large sparkly button to the centre front of the star. Thread the ribbon through the top of one point to make a hanging loop. Decide how long you want the ribbon loop to be and trim the ribbon as necessary. Either tie the ends of the ribbon together in a knot or stitch them to form a loop.

TATE PURSE

Instructions:

Using yarn A, make 64 ch.

Row 1: Skip 3 ch (counts as 1 dc (*UKtr*)), 2 dc (*UKtr*) in next ch, *skip 3 ch, 1 sc (*UKdc*) in next ch, 3 ch, 1 dc (*UKtr*) in next 3 ch, rep from * to last 4 ch, skip 3 ch, 1 sc (*UKdc*) in last ch. Change to yarn B.

Row 2: 3 ch (counts as 1 dc (*UKtr*)), 2 dc (*UKtr*) in first sc (*UKdc*), *skip 3 dc (*UKtr*), 1 sc (*UKdc*) in first of 3-ch, 3 ch, 3 dc (*UKtr*) in next 2-ch sp, rep from * to last 2 dc (*UKtr*), skip 2 dc (*UKtr*), 1 sc (*UKdc*) in top chain of previous round.

Rep row 2 eleven more times, changing colour on every row to yarn C and D then A, B, C and D again, ending last row with colour A.

Fasten off yarn.

Making up

With WS facing, fold the work in half and turn it around, so that the sides are now at the top. Stitch the magnetic flex frame into place by turning a hem over it at the purse opening, and then sew up the sides. You may wish to line the inside of the purse with a piece of felt.

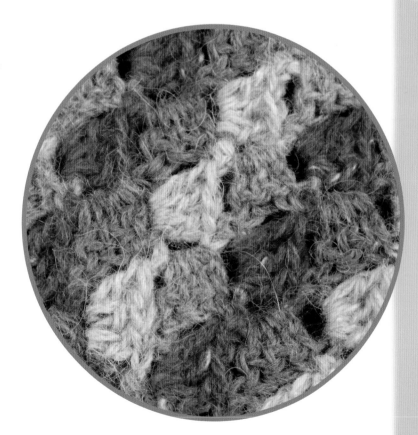

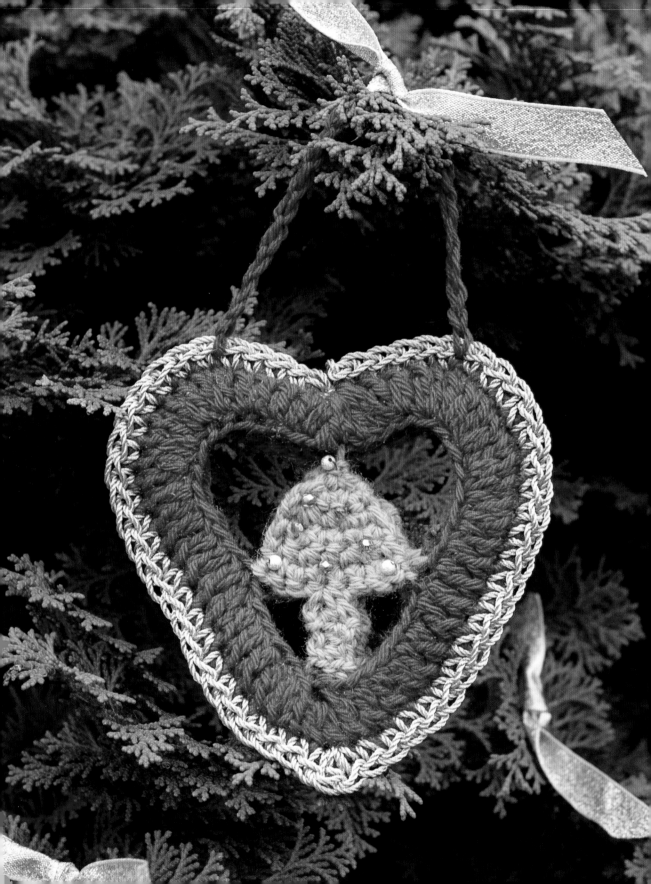

CHRISTMAS TREE HEART

Instructions:

Make two

Using yarn A, ch 40, join with a sl st in first ch, do not twist the chain.

Round 1: Ch 3 (counts as first dc (*UKtr*)), 2 dc (*UKtr*) in the same st, 1 dc (*UKtr*) in each of the next 10 ch, 2 dc (*UKtr*) in each of the next 7 ch, (yrh, insert hook in next ch and pull up a loop, yo and pull through 2 loops on hook) five times, yo and pull through all 6 remaining loops on hook, 2 dc (*UKtr*) in each of the next 7 ch, 1 dc (*UKtr*) in each of the next 10 ch, 2 dc (*UKtr*) in the same st as the first dc (*UKtr*); join with a sl st in the top of the beginning 3-ch.

The tree (make two)

Using yarn B, ch 2 (counts as a st), 2 sc (*UKdc*) in second ch from hook (2 sts).

Row 1: 1 ch, 2 sc (*UKdc*) in each st (4 sts).

Row 2: 1 ch, 2 sc (*UKdc*) in first st, 1 sc (*UKdc*) in next 2 sts, 2 sc (*UKdc*) in last st (6 sts).

Rows 3 and 4: 1 ch, 1 sc (*UKdc*) in each st.

Row 5: 1 ch, 2 sc (*UKdc*) in first st, sc (*UKdc*) in next four sts, 2 sc (*UKdc*) in last st (8 sts).

Fasten off.

Row 6: Rejoin yarn B to fourth st, 1 ch (counts as a st), 1 sc (*UKdc*) in next st (2 sts).

Rows 7–9: 1 ch, 1 sc (*UKdc*) in each st.

Fasten off.

Materials:

Patons Diploma Gold DK (or other light worsted (DK/8-ply)) yarn in red (A) and green (B); 1m/1yd metallic silver thread (C); 50g/131yd/120m

Green sewing thread

Tools:

4mm (US 6, UK 8) crochet hook

Sewing needle

Notions:

A few small silver and green beads

Size:

From bottom point to centre top between lobes: 4¾in (12cm)

Use yarn ends to attach the tree to the centre of the red heart by its three points and the bottom of the trunk.

Pin and block the two pieces carefully with fabric stiffener (starch).

Making up

With WS together, join yarn C to the right of bottom point of heart, 1 ch and sc (*UKdc*) through both layers all around. At the bottom point of the heart, work 1 sc (*UKdc*), 1 hdc (*UKhtr*), 1 sc (*UKdc*) to accentuate the point, sl st to initial ch.

Fasten off, weave in all loose ends.

Attach the beads randomly to both sides of the tree with the sewing needle and thread.

To make the hanger, attach yarn A to the top centre of the right lobe, ch 20 and sl st to top centre of left lobe. Fasten off and weave in loose end.

HELLEBORE GRANNY SQUARE FLOWER

Materials:

Small amounts of No. 3 crochet cotton in mid-green (A), dark green (B), pale green (C) and pink (D); 100g/306yd/280m

Tools:

- 2.5mm (US B/1, UK C/2) crochet hook
- Tapestry needle

Size:

Approx. 4in (10cm) from corner to opposite side

Notes:
The 3-ch picot stitch is worked as follows:
3 ch, sl st into third ch from hook.

Instructions:

Using yarn A, make an adjustable ring, ch 4 (counts as 1 dc (*UKtr*) and 1 ch sp) and work [1 dc (*UKtr*), 1 ch] four times, sl st to third ch of initial 4-ch to form a ring and pull tail end of yarn to close the hole: 5 dc (*UKtr*) each separated by 1 ch. Fasten off.

Round 1: Using yarn B, attach to any 1-ch sp, 1 ch, 5 sc (*UKdc*) into the same sp, work 5 sc (*UKdc*) into each rem 1-ch sp. Fasten off.

Round 2: Using yarn C, attach to the first sc (*UKdc*) of any group of 5 sc (*UKdc*), *3 ch, in next st work 2 dc (*UKtr*), in next st work 1 tr (*UKdtr*), a 3-ch picot, 1 tr (*UKdtr*), in next st work 2 dc (*UKtr*), 3 ch and sl st into next st, sl st into next st, rep from * four times
(5 petals made).

Round 3: Using yarn D and working in the back of the flower, join yarn to a round 1 st between two petals, 5 ch, *sl st to round 1 st between next two petals, 5 ch, rep from * three times, sl st to first st (five 5-ch loops).

Round 4: sl st to loop, [3 ch, 4 dc (*UKtr*), 1 ch] in same loop, *in next loop work [5 dc (*UKtr*), 1 ch], rep from * three times, sl st to third ch of initial 3-ch.

Round 5: sl st to middle of a group of 5 dc (*UKtr*) on previous row, and in centre st of 5 sts, work [3 ch, 3 dc (*UKtr*)], *in next ch-sp work 4 dc (*UKtr*), in next centre st of 5 sts work 4 dc (*UKtr*), rep from * to end, sl st in third ch of initial 3-ch.

Round 6: sl st to middle of group of 4 sts, work [3 ch, 3 dc (*UKtr*)] in sp between centre sts, *in next ch-sp work 4 dc (*UKtr*), in next sp between centre sts of groups of 4 dc (*UKtr*) work 4 dc (*UKtr*), rep from * around, sl st to third ch of initial 3-ch.

Making up

Fasten off and weave in all loose ends. Block to achieve correct pentagonal shape and pin petals out to dry flat.

Materials:

2 balls of Rowan Purelife British Sheep
   Breeds Fine Bouclé
   (or similar worsted/aran
   (10-ply)) yarn in Ecru Masham;
   50g/109yd/100m

Tools:

6mm (US J/10, UK 4) crochet hook

Pompom maker (optional)

Size:

Head circumference 21¼–23in
   (54–58cm)

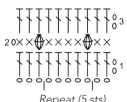

Repeat (5 sts)

WINTER BEANIE

Gauge (tension) sample

10 sts and 8 rows in the bobble pattern using the 6mm (US J/10, UK 4) crochet hook = 4 x 4in (10 x 10cm). Change your hook if necessary to obtain the correct gauge (tension).

Bobble pattern

Work back and forth in rows following the crochet chart. The pattern can be worked over a multiple of 5 sts + 2 for the turning ch. Crochet the 1st dc (*UKtr*) of the 1st row into the 3rd ch from the hook. The numbers on each side show the start of the row. Each row starts with the appropriate number of ch for the st height as shown. Sl st the last stitch in every row into the last stitch of the previous row. Start the row with the st before the repeat, then work the required number of repeats and finish with the st after the repeat. Work rows 1–3 then repeat rows 2–3 until the required length is achieved.

For each bobble, work dc4tog (*UKtr4tog*) into 1 st, then draw the yarn through the 5 loops on the hook together. Crochet the bobbles on WS rows, even though they will appear on RS rows.

Instructions:

Work the hat as a flat piece in rows, starting at the bottom edge and working up to the top point. Join the edges together afterwards to form the centre-back seam.

Begin by working 47 ch loosely (includes 2-ch turning ch). Check that this foundation ch fits around your head.

Row 1: Work 1 dc (*UKtr*) into the 3rd ch from the hook and then into each subsequent ch (45 sts)=.

Rows 2–22: Work in the bobble design following the chart.

Now decrease to shape the top of the hat as follows:

Row 23 (RS row): 2 ch, 4 dc (*UKtr*), dc2tog (*UKtr2tog*), * 3 dc (UKtr), dc2tog (*UKtr2tog*) * , rep from * to * , ending with 4 dc (*UKtr*).

Row 24 (WS row): 1 ch, 2 sc (*UKdc*), * 1 bobble, 3 sc (*UKdc*) *, rep from * to * ending with 1 bobble and 2 sc (*UKdc*).

Row 25: 2 ch, 1 dc (*UKtr*), then work dc2tog (*UKtr2tog*) to the end of the row.

Row 26: 1 ch, * work 1 sc (*UKdc*) then 1 bobble* , rep from * to * ending with 1 sc (*UKdc*).

Row 27: 2 ch, then work dc2tog (*UKtr2tog*) to the end of the row.

Making up

Draw together the remaining sts for the top of the hat using the yarn end, catching in only the decrease stitches. Join the side edges together to form the centre-back seam.

For the hat band, pick up a st in each ch of the foundation ch and work 3 spiral rounds of sc (*UKdc*) (45 sts). Finish the final round with a sl st into the 1st st of the round.

Make a pompom with a diameter of about 2½in (6cm) using the pompom set or by working over cardboard rings (see page 18). Sew the pompom on to the point of the hat.

Materials:

For the single motif:
Small amount of DMC Petra 3 crochet
   cotton in colour of your choice

For the baby blanket:
Sirdar Snuggly DK (or similar light
   worsted (DK/8-ply)) yarn: 1 x 50g
   ball each in pale blue, lemon, pale
   pink and mint green; 3 x 50g balls in
   white; 50g/180yd/165m

Tools:

3mm (US D, UK 10) crochet hook

4mm (US G, UK 8) crochet hook

Size:

Motif is 4½in (11.5cm) in diameter;
   blanket approx. 25½ x 28in (65 x 71cm)

FILET BABY BLANKET

Instructions:

This square is worked in filet crochet. It is charted in squares where each vertical line on the chart represents 1 dc (*UKtr*) and each horizontal line represents 1 ch. Where a square is filled, work 1 dc (*UKtr*) instead of 1 ch.

Row 1: make 30 ch, 1 dc (*UKtr*) into 3rd ch from hook, 1 dc (*UKtr*) into each ch to end, turn.

Row 2: 3 ch, 1 dc (*UKtr*) into next dc (*UKtr*), *1 ch, miss 1 dc (*UKtr*), 1 dc (*UKtr*) in next dc (*UKtr*)*, rep from * to * to last 3 dc (*UKtr*), 1 ch, miss 1 dc (*UKtr*), 1 dc (*UKtr*) in each of last 2 dc (*UKtr*).

Continue to work from the chart until all rows are worked. Fasten off and work in all the ends.

To make the baby blanket

The blanket is worked as 4 vertical strips of 5 squares. The sequence of colours, from right to left, that I have used for each strip is:

Strip A: green, white, pink, white, green.

Strip B: white, blue, white, yellow, white.

Strip C: pink, white, green, white, pink.

Strip D: white, yellow, white, blue, white.

To achieve the white strip in between the coloured squares, work the following rows in white: row 12 of the first square in each strip; rows 1 and 12 of the second, third and fourth squares; and row 1 of the fifth square.

When you have completed all the squares, work the ends in on each one and lay them out on a flat surface in the correct pattern. Carefully sew them together, matching them row for row to maintain a uniform shape.

Edging

Rejoin the white yarn to one corner of the blanket. Work a row of sc (*UKdc*) all round the edges, working into each st across the top and bottom and each row end along both sides. Join with a sl st to beg of round.

Next round: 1 ch, work 1 sc (*UKdc*) into each sc (*UKdc*) all round but work 3 sc (*UKdc*) into each corner as you reach it. Join as before.

Next round: work as previous round, but working 3 sc (*UKdc*) into centre sc (*UKdc*) of each corner.

Next round: as previous round.

Next round: 1 ch, then work a round of sc (*UKdc*) from left to right instead, thus creating a twisted edging (crab stitch), join as before with a sl st. Fasten off. Work in any loose ends.

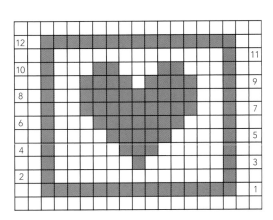

Materials:

I ball each of No. 5 crochet cotton in beige
    and red; 50g/191yd/175m

Small amounts of crochet cotton in dark
    brown and mid green

Black embroidery floss

3 tiny gold beads for hat

Toy stuffing

Sewing threads to match crochet cotton

Tools:

2.5mm (US B1, UK 13) crochet hook

Sewing needle

BERNIE THE CHRISTMAS ELF

Instructions:

Make the bear following the instructions on page 165, using beige for the head, body, arms and legs and dark brown for the muzzle and ears.

Sleeves

Row 1: using red, make 17 ch, 1 dc (*UKtr*) in 3rd ch from hook, 1 dc (*UKtr*) in each ch to end, turn.

Rows 2–4: 3 ch, miss 1 st, 1 dc (*UKtr*) in each st to end.

Row 5: 1 ch, 1 sc (*UKdc*) in each st to end. Fasten off.

Tunic (make 2)

Row 1: using red, make 20 ch, dc (*UKtr*) in 3rd ch from hook, 1 dc (*UKtr*) in each ch to end, turn.

Rows 2 and 3: 3 ch, miss 1 st, 1 dc (*UKtr*) in each dc (*UKtr*) to end.

Row 4: 3 ch, miss 1 st, dc (*UKtr*) 2 tog, dc (*UK tr*) to last 3 sts, dc (*UKtr*) 2 tog, 1 dc (*UKtr*) in last st.

Row 5: sl st across next 4 dc (*UKtr*), 3 ch, 1 dc (*UKtr*) in each dc (*UKtr*) to last 3 dc (*UKtr*), turn.

Row 6: 3 ch, dc (*UKtr*) in each st to end.

Row 7: 3 ch, 1 dc (*UKtr*), 1 hdc (*UKhtr*), 5 sc (*UKdc*), 1 hdc (*UKhtr*), 2 dc (*UKtr*). Fasten off.

Collar

Using green, make 24 ch, 1 sc (*UKdc*) in 2nd ch from hook, dc (*UKtr*) 2 tog over next 2 ch. Fasten off.

*Rejoin yarn to next ch, 3ch, dc (*UKtr*) 2 tog over next 2 ch. Fasten off.* Rep

from * to * along rest of ch, ending 1 sc (*UKdc*) in last ch.

Hat

Row 1: using green, make 26 ch, 1 sc (*UKdc*) in 2nd ch from hook, 1 sc (*UKdc*) in each ch to end, turn.

Row 2: 1 ch, 1 sc (*UKdc*) in each st to end, turn.

Rows 3 and 4: changing to red, 3 ch, miss 1 st, 1 dc (*UKtr*) in each st to end, turn.

Rows 5 and 6: 3 ch, miss 1 st, dc (*UKtr*) 2 tog across row to last st, 1 dc (*UKtr*) in last st, turn.

Rows 7 and 8: 3 ch, 1 dc (*UKtr*) in each st to end.

Row 9: 3 ch, dc (*UKtr*) 2 tog 3 times, 1 dc (*UKtr*) in last tr, turn.

Row 10: 3 ch, miss 1 dc (*UKtr*), 1 dc (*UKtr*) in each st to end. Break yarn.

Run thread through last row, draw up and secure.

Belt

Using green, make ch long enough to go round the bear's waist with a little extra for overlap. Fasten off.

Making up

Work in the ends on all the pieces. Catch the back and front tunic pieces at the shoulder edges to hold them in place. Stitch the sleeves in place. Sew the side and sleeve seams and put the tunic on to the bear. Sew the shoulder seams on either side. Sew the seam on the hat and attach three tiny gold beads to the point. Place the belt around the bear's waist and catch the ends together at the centre back. Place the collar around the bear's neck and join at the centre back. Stretch it slightly to give a good fit.

AFRICAN VIOLETS

Instructions:

With violet crochet cotton, make 4 ch, sl st into a circle.

*1 ch, dc (*UKtr*), tr (*UKdtr*), dc (*UKtr*), 1 ch, sl st, all into loop*, repeat from * to * four more times to make 5 petals.

Tie off the end and press the flower.

Change to yellow crochet cotton and make the central stamen.

3 ch, miss 2 ch, sc (*UKdc*) into ch, sl st into base chain.

Tie off the end.

Insert the yellow stamen into the centre of the flower and sew it in place with sewing thread.

Leaf

With green crochet cotton, make a slip ring, 2 ch, 6 sc (*UKdc*), pull to join, sl st into 2 ch.

Round 1: 2 ch, then 2 dc (*UKtr*) into each sc (*UKdc*) six times, turn.

Round 2: 2 sc (*UKdc*) into each dc (*UKtr*) 12 times, 1 sc (*UKdc*) into 2 ch, 2 dc (*UKtr*) into 2 ch, 1 sc (*UKdc*) into 2 ch, sl st into 2 ch.

Fasten off.

Materials:

Small amounts of No. 3 crochet cotton in violet, yellow and green

Sewing thread

Tools:

2.5mm (US B1, UK 13) crochet hook

Sewing needle

Tapestry needle

185

Bring a forgotten yet much-loved possession back to life with these brightly coloured flowers.

FESTIVE WREATH

Instructions:

Using light green crochet cotton, make 50 ch.

Row 1: Work 2 dc (*UKtr*) into 3rd ch from hook, 3 dc (*UKtr*) into each ch to end. As you work, the crochet will twirl into a tight corkscrew shape.

Use dark green cotton to make another twist in the same way.

Making up

Secure both the light green and dark green crochet twists together at one end, then twine the strips around each other, folding the coils inside one another as you do so, until you get a neat double coil. Join the two ends together firmly.

Glue the holly berry embellishments on the coil at random, tucking them inside the twists. Glue the ribbon bow and bell at the top of the wreath to cover the join where the ends of the twists meet.

Thread the ribbon through the top of the wreath to make a hanging loop. Decide how long you want the ribbon loop to be and trim the ribbon as necessary. Either tie the ends of the ribbon together in a knot or stitch them to form a loop.

Materials:

1 ball each of No. 5 crochet cotton in dark green and light green; 50g/191yd/175m

3 small holly berry embellishments

20in (0.5m) of narrow green satin ribbon

Gold ribbon bow or a short length of gold ribbon to tie in a bow

Gold bell

Craft glue

Green sewing thread (optional)

Tools:

Size 2mm (US B1, UK 14) crochet hook

Sewing needle

Size:

Approx. 2¾in (7cm) in diameter

LOTTIE PURSE

Instructions:

Make 2

With 3.5mm (US E/4, UK 9) crochet hook make 5 ch, join with sl st to first ch to form a ring.

Round 1: 3 ch (counts as 1 dc (*UKtr*)), 1 dc (*UKtr*) into ring, *1 ch, 2 dc (*UKtr*) into ring, rep from * four more times, 1 ch, sl st in top of 3 ch.

Round 2: sl st to first dc (*UKtr*) and ch sp, 3 ch (counts as 1 dc (*UKtr*)), [1 dc (*UKtr*), 1 ch, 2 dc (*UKtr*)] into same sp, 1 ch, *[2dc (*UKtr*), 1 ch, 2 dc (*UKtr*)] into next ch sp, 1 ch, rep from * four more times, sl st in top of 3 ch.

Round 3: sl st to first dc (*UKtr*) and ch sp, 3 ch (counts as 1 dc (*UKtr*)), 2 dc (*UKtr*) into same ch sp, 1 ch, *3 dc (*UKtr*) into next ch sp, 1 ch, rep from * to end, sl st in top of 3 ch.

Round 4: sl st to next 2 dc (*UKtr*) and ch sp, 3 ch (counts as 1 dc (*UKtr*)), 2 dc (*UKtr*) into same ch sp, 1 ch, *3 dc (*UKtr*) into next ch sp, 1 ch, rep from * to end, sl st in top of 3 ch.

Round 5: sl st to next 2 dc (*UKtr*) and ch sp, 3 ch (counts as 1 dc (*UKtr*)), 1 dc (*UKtr*) into same ch sp, 1 ch, *[2dc (*UKtr*), 1 ch, 2 dc (*UKtr*)] into next ch sp, 1 ch, rep from * five more times, 2 dc (*UKtr*) into next ch sp.

Fasten off yarn.

Shell edge

With RS facing, attach yarn to top of 3 ch at beg of last round, 1 ch, *6 dc (*UKtr*) into next ch sp, 1 sc (*UKdc*) into next ch sp, rep from * five more times, 6 dc (*UKtr*) into next ch sp, 1 sc (*UKdc*) to top of last dc (*UKtr*) from previous round.

Making up

Weave in all loose ends. Attach the narrower parts of the circle to the purse clasp and sew together around the shell edging. Sew the lining to the inside of the purse, leaving a ½in (1cm) seam allowance.

Materials:

1 ball of 4-ply yarn in red; 50g/197yd/180m

2 x pieces of fabric for lining, approx. 4in (10cm) in diameter (optional)

Hook:

3.5mm (US E/4, UK 9) crochet hook

Notions:

1 x rounded purse clasp approx. 3¼in (8cm) wide

Size:

Approx. 4¾in (12cm) at the widest point and 4in (10cm) in height

HEART STRING

Instructions:

Make 2 for each heart.

Round 1: With yarn colour of your choice, make an adjustable ring, ch 3, and work into the ring 6 sc (*UKdc*), 1 dc (*UKtr*), 6 sc (*UKdc*), 3ch, sl st. Gently pull the tail end of the yarn to close the ring (but leave a small gap, as your final sl st will be made into the centre) and the heart shape will appear.

Round 2: 3 ch, miss the 3-ch from previous round, 3 sc (*UKdc*) into the first st, 1 sc (*UKdc*) in each of the next 2 sts, 1 hdc (*UKhtr*) in each of the next 3 sts, [1 dc (*UKtr*), 1 tr (*UKdtr*), 1 dc (*UKtr*)] into the next st (this is the bottom point of the heart), 1 hdc (*UKhtr*) in each of the next 3 sts, 1 sc (*UKdc*) in each of the next 2 sts, 3 sc (*UKdc*) in the last st, ch 3 and sl st in the centre of the heart.

Edging

First, tug the yarn tail again to make sure the centre hole is closed properly, as you will now be stuffing the heart. This will prevent any toy stuffing poking through.

Holding two hearts tog with WS facing, join yarn to the right of the bottom point, ch 1 and sc (*UKdc*) in each st through both layers. You may need to work 2 sc (*UKdc*) into one or two sts on the curves of the heart lobes so that the stitches do not pull. At the bottom point of the heart, work 1 sc (*UKdc*), 1 dc (*UKtr*), 1 sc (*UKdc*) into the middle st, then sl st into initial ch. Fasten off and weave in all loose ends.

Materials:

Small amounts of Rowan pure wool DK (or similar light worsted (DK/8-ply)) in maroon, pink and mushroom; 50g/142yd/130m

Sewing thread

Toy stuffing

Tools:

4mm (US 6, UK 8) crochet hook

Sewing needle

Notions:

8 small bell beads

3 hanging decorations in toning colours

Size:

23¼in (59cm) from top of loop to bottom of hanging decoration

Making up

Choose a colour for the hanging chain and connect the six hearts tog by joining yarn to the middle of the heart lobes, make 6 ch and join to bottom point of next heart. Repeat to join all hearts tog. To make the hanging loop, join yarn to the middle of the heart lobes on the top heart, make 16 ch and rejoin to the middle. Fasten off.

Sew a bell bead to the bottom of the top five hearts, and three to the bottom of the last heart. Attach some hanging decorations with gold and maroon beads to the bottom heart with some yarn.

The motifs for this baby cube toy were worked in *Cygnet Seriously Chunky* acrylic yarn using a combination of cream (A), candyfloss (B) and bluebell (C) – yardage: 100g/52yd/48m.

Make six squares in the colour combinations of your choice. Block if desired. Join five of the squares together by working single crochet (UKdc) through the back loops of the sts, with WS together. Join the sixth square by one side only, gently ease a cube insert (sized to fit your joined motifs and with a jingly bell in the middle) into the shape and, using a tapestry needle, stitch the remaining three sides closed. Fasten off and weave in loose ends.

ANEMONE GRANNY SQUARE FLOWER

Materials:

Small amounts of crochet cotton in pink (A), fuchsia pink (B) and pale green (C); 100g/306yd/280m

Tools:

2.5mm (US B/1, UK C/2) crochet hook

Tapestry needle

Size:

Approx. 3in (8cm) from corner to opposite side

Instructions:

Using yarn A, ch 4 and join with sl st to first ch to form a ring.

Round 1: 3 ch, 11 dc (*UKtr*) in ring, sl st to third ch of initial 3-ch (12 sts). Fasten off.

Round 2: Join B to a space between sts, 3 ch, 1 dc (*UKtr*) in same space, 2 dc (*UKtr*) in each sp between sts around, sl st to third ch of initial 3-ch. Fasten off (24 sts).

Round 3: Join C to sp between a pair of dc (*UKtr*), [3 ch, 2 dc (*UKtr*)], 1 ch in same sp, *form corner by missing 3 dc (*UKtr*), work [3 dc (*UKtr*), 2 ch, 3 dc (*UKtr*)] into next sp, miss 3 dc (*UKtr*), work into next sp [3 dc (*UKtr*), 1 ch] rep from * twice, miss three dc (*UKtr*), work [3 dc (*UKtr*), 2 ch, 3 dc (*UKtr*)] in next sp, 1 ch and sl st to third ch of initial 3-ch.

Making up

Fasten off and weave in all loose ends. Block carefully to achieve a regular square.

SUGARCRAFT KNOW-HOW

Materials

The main materials you will need to make all the sugar decorations in this section are:

Modelling paste Some of the models use modelling paste – fondant (sugarpaste) strengthened with CMC (cellulose gum) or gum tragacanth. Use 8oz (250g) fondant (sugarpaste) to approximately half a teaspoon of the gum. This is used when parts need to dry harder, for example, long beaks and parts that need to stand. Leave for a few hours for the gum to develop before using.

Fondant (sugarpaste) This paste is commercially available as coloured fondant (sugarpaste). White fondant (sugarpaste) can also be coloured with strong edible food colours from sugarcraft shops and some supermarkets. It is not advisable to use liquid colours when making dark or bold colours, as this makes the fondant (sugarpaste) sticky and unworkable.

Mexican paste This is also known as flower paste or gum paste. It is used to make anything that needs to dry quickly and hold its shape, such as flowers.

Sugar glue This is made by slowly warming ½oz (15g) of fondant (sugarpaste) and ½fl oz (15ml) of water in the microwave until it boils. When cool, it is ready for use. Sugar glue keeps well in a small screw-top jar.

Strong gel paste colours These are used for mixing in to white modelling paste to make solid colours.

Icing sugar and cornstarch (cornflour) These can both be used when rolling out paste to stop it sticking. Use it sparingly as they will dry paste out too much if you are not careful.

White fat This stops the paste sticking to the board if it is too dry when rolling out.

Other materials you may need are:

Chenille sticks Also called pipe cleaners, these can be obtained in various colours from craft shops.

Clear piping gel This is used to glue and gloss.

Confectioner's glaze This will allow you to give a shiny finish to painted noses.

Edible candy sticks These can be either bought or made and dried in advance. Mix 9oz (250g) of fondant (sugarpaste) or royal icing with half a teaspoon of Tylose powder, CMC or gum tragacanth. Roll into thin sausages, cut to short lengths and allow to dry for at least 24 hours or longer.

Edible food colour powder Available in plain and pearl colours, these are brushed onto the surface to add soft colour or an iridescent sheen.

Edible food colouring pens These are useful for drawing on features.

Edible metallic paint Gold and silver paint can be used to great effect.

Edible sprinkles These are used for decoration.

Edible wafer paper This can be used to make birds' wings and other delicate components.

Food grade alcohol This is used mixed with edible powder food colour, for painting.

Edible glitter Use only glitter labelled 'for food contact', and remember to remind people if the figures you make are non-edible.

Styrofoam (polystyrene) balls These can be found in most craft shops or art shops.

Leaf gelatine sheets These can be used in conjunction with modelling paste to form transparent areas.

Royal icing This is used to pipe hair on to figures, and as an adhesive.

Small black edible sugar pearls These make good eyes and noses.

Vegetable cooking oil To stop the paste sticking to your hands and tools, rub a small amount of this into your hands and your work surface.

Tools

You will need these basic tools for nearly all the projects in this book. They can all be obtained from sugarcraft shops or online cake decorating suppliers:

A **pointed tool**, a **smiley tool** or **drinking straw**, **paintbrushes** for dusting paste or attaching pieces together, a **texture frilling tool**, and a **ball tool**, a **dogbone tool** and a **Dresden tool**. Note that some of the tools are double-ended – the pointed tool has one pointed and one rounded end, for example.

A **non-stick work board** This makes it easier to roll out the paste without it moving. Place a **non-slip mat** underneath to prevent your board from moving.

Small non-stick rolling pin This is used for rolling out your paste. There are many different sizes and patterns of **textured rolling pins**. They can be obtained from cake decorating suppliers or online.

Small pair of scissors These are used to cut paste or ribbons.

Small, thin palette knife Use this to release paste from your board.

Cutters Made of plastic or metal, these come in various shapes such as ovals, circles or hearts. Small **blossom cutters** are easy-to-use flower-shaped cutters that come in many sizes. A **Garrett frill cutter** can make large circle frills.

Cocktail sticks Used to support pieces of sugar items while drying, and for texturing.

Craft knife A sharp blade is essential in order to ensure safe cutting.

Mini digital scales Ideal for weighing out small amounts of paste.

Multi-mould This can be used to make a tiny crown, wings, bow, a tiny flower, a tiny faceted star and many other small items.

Small pieces of foam These help support sugar items whilst they are drying.

A **stamen** This is a round bead attached to a stick and can be used when making flowers or for eyes.

Icing tubes Used to make circles, buttons or dots.

Small wire cutters Used to cut cocktail sticks, chenille sticks or wires to the required length.

Clay gun, tea strainer or **sieve** Used to make very thin strands of fondant (sugarpaste) for hair or fluff, simply push the fondant (sugarpaste) through the mesh.

You will also need some more specific tools for making some of the decorations:

Butterfly wings can be made in Mexican (flower/gum) paste using a cutter, or bought ready made from card.

Bell moulds come in many different sizes and can be obtained from sugarcraft shops or online cake decorating suppliers.

Bulbous cone tool Push this into the centre of a flower to open up the centre.

Cutting wheel This is used for cutting shapes from rolled fondant (sugarpaste).

Design wheel For adding large stitch and zigzag patterns and lines.

Dowel When making mini shoes, shoe soles are laid over a pen or pencil, acting as a dowel to create the high-heeled shape.

Leaf cutters These are available in a vast array of shapes and sizes, in metal or plastic.

Food-grade kebab, barbecue or cake-pop sticks.

Kitchen paper This is used when dusting and drying flowers and leaves.

Leaf veiners The leaf is placed inside and the veiners are squashed together to create a veined surface on the front and back of the leaf.

Lustre spray Pearl, gold, bronze, pink – this is spray food colour with sparkle.

195

Mexican foam balling pad Use this when softening, cupping and shaping the edges of petals.

Music stave cutter Useful for cutting thin strips of modelling paste or fondant (sugarpaste).

Piping bag and tubes These are used for piping leaves, stems, petals and other parts.

Ribbon Use this to back flower sprays and fill in gaps.

Small **drinking straw** This should be cut off at an angle, and is used for making mouths and closed eyes. Small **plain piping tubes** are also useful for cutting tiny circles for eyes and other small features or decorations.

Small long-nosed pliers Bending wires in place is much easier and safer with this tool.

Stem tape This is a stretchy self-sticking paper tape used to cover wires for flower making. Attach stamens to the ends of wires and to bind flowers together into sprays, posies and arrangements. It can also be used to make stamens.

Stitching wheel This is used to add a stitched effect.

Tape cutter This cuts stem tape down into thinner widths for ease of use.

Tapered and serrated cone tools Push these into the centre of a flower to mark a star shape or marking guidelines.

Tweezers Useful for picking up tiny pieces of paste.

White alcohol Mix this with food colours for painting. Alcohol evaporates quickly, ensuring no surface damage is done to the icing. You can use dipping solution, rejuvenator spirit, lemon extract or clear vanilla essence instead.

Wires Paper-covered wire is good for making flower stems, the thickness of which is measured in gauge (g), 18g being the thickest and 33g being the thinnest. Choose a gauge of wire to suit the weight and size of your flower.

Modelling paste recipe (for 9oz/250g)

If you want to make your own modelling paste, simply follow this recipe:

1 Break 9oz (250g) of fondant (sugarpaste) into small pieces. Sprinkle ½–1tsp (2.5–5ml) CMC, gum tragacanth or Tylose edible gum powder over the fondant (sugarpaste), depending on how stiff you want it; the more powder, the firmer the paste.

2 Spread white vegetable fat (shortening) on your hands and knead the gum into the paste. Knead in food colouring if the paste was not coloured before.

3 Cover with plastic wrap and leave to rest for a few hours or overnight. Always knead well before working with it and rolling it out. Add white vegetable fat if it feels dry. Roll out on a cutting mat using a non-stick roller.

Basic shapes

Several of the models in this section use the same basic body and head shapes. Follow the instructions on this page to make them. Individual projects will indicate when this type of basic body or head should be used.

Basic bodies

1 Roll 1½oz (45g) of modelling paste into a ball.

2 Shape the paste into a cone 2½in (6.5cm) tall.

3 Insert a 3⅛in (8cm) cocktail stick through the middle of the cone to the base for support. The top of the cocktail stick will support the head. Make two holes in the front for the legs to fit in.

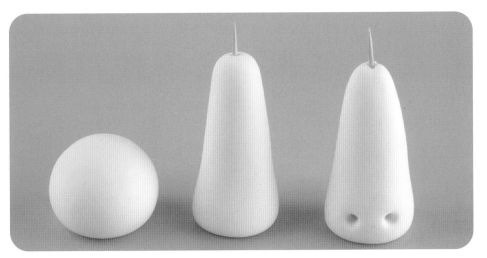

Heads

1 Roll ⅔oz (20g) of modelling paste into a smooth ball. Make a small hole in the middle of the face ready for the nose.

2 Make a small round-ended cone of paste for the nose and insert it into the hole using a small amount of sugar glue.

3 Use a smiley tool or drinking straw to make the mouth.

4 Make two holes for the eyes and leave to dry.

Eyes

1 These are made using stamens (see below). Insert them into the head and leave to dry. If you cannot obtain stamens, you can use two very small balls of white paste for the eyes.

2 Use a fine black fibre-tip pen to mark the pupils onto the stamens or paste.

Changing the colour of the rose to white makes it resemble a Christmas rose. Spray it with pearl lustre spray for added Christmas sparkle.

Materials:

Mexican (flower/gum) paste: white, green, yellow

Powdered food colour: pink, yellow, green

Royal icing: white

Tools:

Rose petal cutter (largest from set of 4)

Medium rose leaf plunger cutter: 1¼in (30mm)

Daisy marguerite plunger cutter: 1in (27mm)

Paintbrush: ½in (12mm) flat

Mini modelling tool

Flower former

Mexican foam balling pad

Ball tool

CHRISTMAS ROSE

Instructions:

1 On a non-stick surface, roll out some white Mexican (flower/gum) paste quite thinly. Cut out a rose petal using the largest single rose petal cutter (A).

2 Place the petal on a Mexican foam balling pad, then rub a ball or bone tool around the edge of the petal to soften and shape. Then curl the upper edges of the petal back by rolling them from the outer edge inwards with a mini modelling tool (B).

3 Flip the petal over and cup it using a large ball tool, rubbing it around in a circular motion in the centre of the petal (C). Prepare a further four petals in the same way.

4 While the petals are still soft, stick them together with sugar glue, lining the points up at the bottom and the left edge of each petal positioned about halfway across the previous one (D). Once you have all five in position, bend them around, so that you can stick the first petal to the last to complete the circle. Lay in a flower former to dry.

5 Use the daisy cutter to cut out a daisy shape from white Mexican (flower/gum) paste (E).

6 Roll each of the petals from side to side with a mini modelling tool to widen and thin, then use the scissors to cut each petal of the daisy shape in half (F).

7 Take a pea-sized ball of yellow Mexican (flower/gum) paste and roll it into a cone shape using the heel of your hand (G).

8 Take a small pair of scissors and repeatedly snip into the surface of the cone at the bulbous end to create the stamens. Cut off the tapered end of the cone so that the base is now flat (H).

9 To complete the stamen centre, stick the stamens into the centre of the prepared daisy shape with a little sugar glue (I).

10 Stick the prepared centre into the middle of the flower with sugar glue. Place in a flower former to dry (J).

11 Use the flat brush to colour the centre with a little yellow and green powdered food colour and the edge of the petals with pink. Arrange on an oval plaque with three rose leaves made from green Mexican (flower/gum) paste.

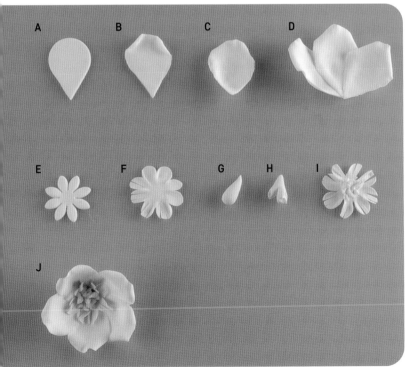

Materials:

1oz (30g) pink
    modelling paste

Edible sugar candy sticks

½oz (15g) white
    modelling paste

Very small amount
    of white fondant
    (sugarpaste)

Edible black sugar pearls

Clear piping gel (optional)

Tools:

Stitching wheel

Dresden tool

Water brush

Thin palette knife

Tea strainer/small
    sieve

Multi-mould (tiny bow)

PRETTY POODLE

Instructions:

1 Make two tiny bows using the pink modelling paste in the tiny bow mould.

2 Use the rest of the pink modelling paste to shape a 1½in (4cm) heart cushion. Mark round the edge with the stitching wheel.

3 Push in two 1¼in (3cm) candy sticks at the angle shown, then two in vertically, for the legs. Make sure that the tops of the sticks have only 1¼in (3cm) between the front and back pairs to allow space for the body. Trim the tops of the vertical legs to be level with the tops of the back legs.

4 Shape ⅙oz (5g) of white modelling paste to a 1¼in (3cm) sausage for the body. Push in a short edible candy stick vertically for the neck, and a shorter piece at an angle for the tail.

5 Shape ¹⁄₁₀oz (2.5g) white modelling paste to a long pear shape for the head. Turn up the narrow end slightly for the nose. Pinch and shape the sides of the muzzle to make them hang down more. Shape the fat end of the head

gently to form a higher forehead. Mark the eyes and nose with a Dresden tool and insert edible black sugar pearls. Dampen the top of the neck and press the head into place.

6 Dampen the tops of the legs and push the body into place, head end above the vertical legs. Leave to dry overnight.

7 Dampen the areas where the fluff will go. Push white fondant (sugarpaste) through the tea strainer or sieve to make fluff. When you have the length you want, cut it off with a knife and attach it to the dampened areas on the dog. Press into place with a Dresden tool; don't press with fingers as you may flatten the fluff. If you have trouble getting it to stay on, use clear piping gel as a glue instead of dampening with water.

8 For the ears, make two small ovals. Dampen the sides of the head and attach them, hanging down. Dampen the ears and cut and attach some fluff. Attach the tiny pink bows at the tops of the ears.

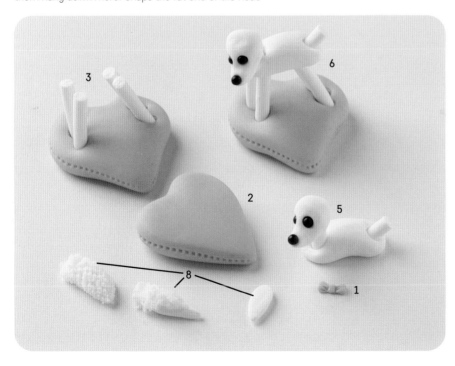

Materials:

4¼oz (120g) brown or chocolate modelling paste

Small amounts of cream, black and blue modelling paste

Small amount of tangerine Mexican (flower/gum) paste

One chenille stick (pipe cleaner), stripy if possible

Two large white stamens

Cocktail stick

Tools:

Basic tools (see page 195)

Fine black fibre-tip pen

Cutters: 2⅜in (6cm) circle, 1¾in (4.5cm) circle, small oval and small circle

Sugar glue

Small pair of scissors

Rolling pin

Instructions:

1 Make a basic body in brown as shown on page 197, then make two holes in the front for the legs using the pointed tool.

2 Roll a small amount of of cream paste into a smooth ball, then flatten it into an thin oval for the tummy. Glue it in place with sugar glue then leave to dry.

3 Make the head as shown on page 197 using brown paste, then make two holes for the eyes with the pointed stick.

LION

4 Insert stamens for the eyes. Using a fine black fibre-tip pen, mark the pupils with dots. Leave to dry.

5 Use the cream paste and small oval cutter to make a small flat oval shape for his muzzle and glue it on to the front of the face with sugar glue. Make a small hole at the top of the oval for the nose with the pointed tool.

6 Use a straw to make the mouth, then add two small balls of cream paste for the cheeks. Glue the cheeks in place with sugar glue, then use a cocktail stick or scriber to make little holes. Leave to dry.

7 Make a small cone of black paste and insert this into the nose hole using a small amount of sugar glue.

8 To make the ears, roll 1/12oz (2g) of brown paste into a smooth ball, then cut it in half and roll each piece into a ball again. Push the rounded end of a pointed tool into one ball but do not take the tool out. Add sugar glue to the bottom part of the ear and place it on the top of the head firmly. Remove the tool. Repeat with the other ear then leave to dry.

9 For the arms, roll 2/3oz (20g) of brown paste into a smooth ball, cut it in half and roll each half into a sausage shape equal to the length of the body. Attach with a little sugar glue.

10 To make the paws and feet, roll 1/2oz (16g) of brown paste into a ball and cut it into four using the scissors. Shape each quarter into a flat oval disc. Mark each as shown with a cocktail stick and attach to the arms using sugar glue.

11 Cut an 3¼in (8cm) length of chenille stick (pipe cleaner). Apply glue to each end. Attach a foot to one end and push the other end into the body to make a leg. Repeat to make the other leg. Bend into shape when dry.

12 Roll out the tangerine paste with the rolling pin, but not too thinly. Make the mane by cutting out a circle using a 2⅜in (6cm) cutter. Next, cut out the middle, slightly off centre, using the 1¾in (4.5cm) circle cutter.

13 Snip with scissors all the way round to make a fringe, then cut the circle across the bottom edge. Glue the mane in place behind the ears. Repeat with a second circle of fringe, and support with foam if necessary.

14 Cut out small circles of blue paste for the buttons using the small circle cutter. Attach them with a little sugar glue, then mark them with a cocktail stick.

203

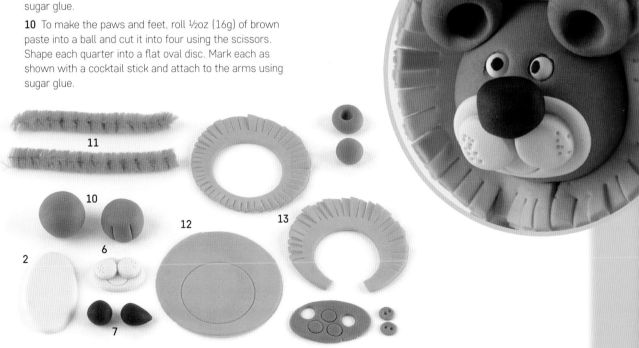

9/10

12

13

14

11

7

4

15

CHOIRBOY

Materials:

2oz (55g) red modelling paste

⁵⁄₆oz (26g) flesh-coloured paste

Small amounts of black and brown modelling paste

Small amount of white Mexican (flower/gum) paste

One beige chenille stick (pipe cleaner)

Gold glitter

Pale pink dusting powder

Cocktail sticks

Tools:

Cutters: circle cutters, star

Fine black fibre-tip pen

No. 2 icing nozzle

Sugar glue

Cocktail stick

Instructions:

1 Make a red body as shown on page 197 and insert a 3¼in (8cm) cocktail stick. Make two holes in the front for the legs using the pointed tool.

2 Roll ⅔oz (20g) of flesh-coloured paste into a smooth ball for the head. Use a pointed tool to make a hole for the nose and use the smiley tool to mark the mouth.

3 Roll a small ball of paste into a cone for the nose. Using a little glue, insert the narrow end into the hole in the head.

4 For the ears, roll ¹⁄₁₆oz (1g) of flesh-coloured paste into a ball. Cut it in half and roll each piece into a smaller ball. Push the rounded end of a pointed tool into one of the balls. Add glue to the bottom part of the ear and secure it firmly to the side of the head. Remove the tool and repeat with the other ear. Leave to dry.

5 When the head is completely dry, mark the eyes as shown with a fine black fibre-tip pen. Dust the cheeks with pink dusting powder.

6 Cut two 3in (7.5cm) lengths of beige chenille stick (pipe cleaner) for the legs.

7 To make the shorts, cut a ⅓oz (10g) ball of red paste in half and roll each piece into a smaller ball. Insert a chenille stick (pipe cleaner) through the middle of one ball and roll it into a cylinder as shown. Lightly glue one end of the chenille stick (pipe cleaner) and push it into the body, then lightly glue the small ball of red paste and press it on to the body. Repeat with the other leg.

8 For the shoes, cut a ⁵⁄₁₂oz (12g) ball of black paste in half to make two flat ovals. Lightly glue the remaining end of the chenille stick (pipe cleaner) and attach the shoe. Repeat with the other shoe.

9 Use a large circle cutter to cut out a circle of white paste to make the lower skirt. Frill the outer edge with the rounded end of the pointed tool, then make decorative holes using the small end of the icing nozzle. With the large end, cut out a hole in the middle. Add a little glue around the middle of the body, then pull the skirt down over the cocktail stick, supporting it with foam if necessary.

10 Cut out a second skirt and frill the outer edge. Glue the top of the cocktail stick and pull the skirt down carefully over the body.

11 Roll ⅛oz (3g) of flesh-coloured paste into a ball and cut it in half to make two oval hands. Add a little sugar glue to each end of an 4⅜in (11cm) beige chenille stick (pipe cleaner), and attach the hands. Bend the chenille stick (pipe cleaner) around the back of the cocktail stick and glue it in place.

12 Roll out some white paste and cut two medium size blossoms for the neck frills. Lightly frill the edges, add glue to the cocktail stick, then place the frills on individually. Press down firmly at the front and the back, over the chenille stick (pipe cleaner), before gluing the head on firmly.

13 For the hair, roll out a small circle of brown paste, and lightly glue it on to the top of the head. Mark the hair by pulling the tip of a cocktail stick down over the sugar paste hair. Try not to cross the lines over.

14 For the top hair, roll out a 1³⁄₁₆ x ⅝in (3cm x 1.5cm) rectangle of brown paste, make small cuts along one edge, and roll it up tightly before placing it on the top of the head as shown. Secure with a little glue.

15 Cut out a star from white paste and glue gold glitter over it. Once dry, bring the arms and hands down into position and glue the star to his hands.

Materials:

⅓oz (10g) flesh-coloured
    fondant (sugarpaste)

Brown fondant (sugarpaste) or
    modelling chocolate:
    ⅓oz (10g) for the body,
    ⅓oz (10g) for the legs,
    ⅙oz (5g) for the arms and
    ⅙oz (5g) for the hat

⅓oz (10g) mixed red, yellow and orange fondant
    (sugarpaste) (not mixed too thoroughly)

Candy stick

Tiny amount of black fondant
    (sugarpaste) for the eyes

Tools:

Oak leaf cutters

Non-stick rolling pin

Small drinking straw

Thin palette knife

Plastic sandwich bag

Water brush

Dresden tool or cocktail stick

WINTER FAIRY

Instructions:

1 Make an egg shape of brown fondant (sugarpaste) for the body with a candy stick for support, slightly sticking out. Lay the body on its side.

2 For the legs, divide the piece of brown fondant (sugarpaste). Roll each piece to a long carrot shape about twice the length of the body. Bend in the middle for the knees.

3 For the shoes, make two pea-sized pieces of the mixed fondant (sugarpaste) and shape each one to a point. Dampen the ends of the legs and attach the shoes. Attach the legs to the body.

4 For the arms, divide the piece of brown fondant (sugarpaste) and form two carrot shapes, slightly longer than the body. Bend to form the elbows, and flatten the hands. Attach to the body.

5 Roll out some of the mixed fondant (sugarpaste). Cut out at least seven oak leaves for the skirt, one for the sleeve and four for the wings. Attach to the body.

6 Make the head from a ball of fondant (sugarpaste) with a slight indentation in the middle and two tiny teardrop shapes for the ears and a tiny pinhead piece for the nose.

7 For the hair, make lots of small carrot-shaped pieces of mixed fondant (sugarpaste). Dampen the head and attach the strands of hair with the pointed ends towards the face and neck. When the head is covered with enough strands of hair, dampen the end of the candy stick neck and attach the head.

8 Form a large acorn cup for the hat from a slightly larger than pea-sized piece of brown paste. Texture the surface with a cocktail stick. Make a small hole in the middle. Stick the acorn cup hat on the back of the head. Make a small stalk from brown fondant (sugarpaste) and attach it to the middle of the acorn cup.

These small African birds are renowned for showing affection to their mates, so spread the love with a little fondant (sugarpaste)!

LOVEBIRDS

Materials:

⅓oz (10g) green
  fondant (sugarpaste)
Small amounts of yellow,
  orange, red, black and white
  fondant (sugarpaste)

Tools:

Dresden tool/cocktail stick
No. 2 piping tube

Instructions:

1 For the wings, take a pea-sized amount of green fondant (sugarpaste) for each wing and shape it to a pointed cone. Mark it with the Dresden tool or a cocktail stick to look like feathers.

2 To make the body, attach a large pea-sized piece of yellow and one of orange fondant (sugarpaste) to the ball of green. Dampen if necessary. Shape to a 2½in (6cm) cone, smoothing the joins between the colours with your fingers. Roll the fat end between your fingers to form a neck. Curve the body to stand up

and mark on the tail feathers with the Dresden tool or a cocktail stick. Attach the wings.

3 Mark the eye sockets on to the head with a piping tube, and attach two tiny eyes using two balls of black fondant (sugarpaste).

4 Make an indentation where the beak will go. Shape a small, red pointed cone of fondant (sugarpaste) and attach it to the head in the indentation. Curve the tip of the beak down and mark on the nostrils.

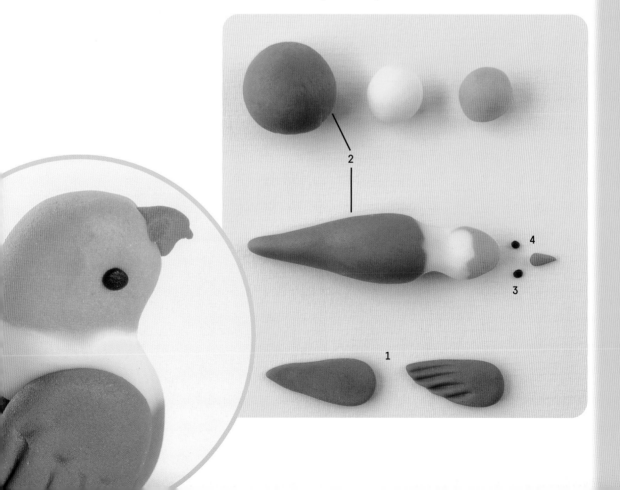

Materials:

2¾oz (80g) red modelling paste

⅚oz (25g) flesh-coloured modelling paste

⅔oz (20g) black modelling paste

Small amount of white Mexican (flower/gum) paste

Gold paint

Pale pink dusting powder

One red chenille stick (pipe cleaner)

White royal icing

No. 2 icing nozzle and piping bag

Tools:

Basic tools

Cutters: small square, 1½in (4cm) oval, 1³⁄₁₆in (3cm) circle

Fine black fibre-tip pen

Craft knife

Sugar glue

Paintbrush

Instructions:

1 Make a red body as shown on page 197 and insert a 3¼in (8cm) cocktail stick. Make two holes in the front for the legs using the pointed tool.

2 Roll ⅔oz (20g) of flesh-coloured paste into a smooth ball for the head. Use a pointed tool to make a hole for the nose and use the smiley tool to mark the mouth.

SANTA CLAUS

3 Roll a small ball of flesh-coloured paste into a cone for the nose. Using a little glue, insert the narrow end into the hole in the head.

4 For the ears, cut a 1/16oz (1g) ball of flesh-coloured paste in half and roll each piece into a smaller ball. Push the rounded end of a pointed tool into one ball. Glue the bottom part of the ear and place it firmly at the side of the head. Remove the tool and repeat with the other ear. Leave to dry. When the head is completely dry, mark the eyes with a fine black fibre-tip pen and dust the cheeks with pale pink dusting powder.

5 Cut two 3in (7.5cm) lengths of chenille stick (pipe cleaner) for the legs.

6 To make the trousers, cut a 5/12oz (12g) ball of red paste in half and roll each piece into a smaller ball. Insert a length of chenille stick (pipe cleaner) through the middle of one ball and roll it into a cylinder. Repeat with the other leg. Lightly glue one end of each chenille stick (pipe cleaner) and push into the body, then glue the small ball of red paste and press further on to the body. Repeat with the other leg.

7 For the boots, cut a 1/2oz (15g) ball of black paste in half. Roll each half into a sausage shape and turn up one end to make the boot. Glue the remaining end of the chenille stick (pipe cleaner) and attach the boot. Repeat with the other boot.

8 Roll 1/5oz (6g) of red paste into a ball and cut it in half to make two oval mittens. Add sugar glue to each end of a 4¾in (12cm) length of red chenille stick (pipe cleaner) and attach a mitten to each end. Bend the chenille stick (pipe cleaner) around the back of the cocktail stick and glue in place. Shape the arms and hands into position when dry.

9 To make the collar, cut out a circle of red paste using the 1³/16in (3cm) cutter. Make a small cut in the paste as shown. Using a little glue, place the collar over the cocktail stick. Push the head on firmly.

10 To make the beard, cut out an oval from white paste, trim off the end using the end of the oval cutter, and cut the removed part in half to make the moustache as shown. Secure the beard and moustache in place with a little royal icing.

11 To represent the fur and hair, pipe small circles of white royal icing on the Father Christmas as shown.

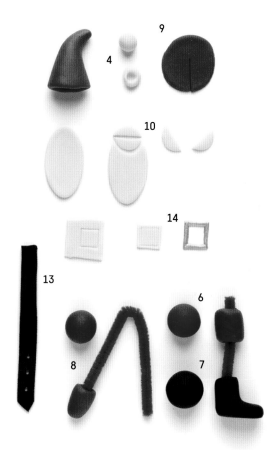

12 Roll out 1/3oz (10g) of red paste into a ball. Make it into a cone by opening out the middle with a large pointed tool and stretching the top to a point as shown, then glue the hat to the top of the head.

13 Roll a ³/8 x 4in (1 x 10cm) strip of black paste for a belt. Cut holes along one end with the narrow end of an icing nozzle and cut that end into a point. Glue in place.

14 For the buckle, roll out a small amount of white Mexican (flower/gum) paste and cut a small square. Leave the square in the paste. Using a craft knife, cut a second square around the outer edge of the first one. Lift both squares using a palette knife and remove the inner one. Make a very small oval of white paste for the hook inside the buckle. Paint both gold. When dry attach to the belt with sugar glue.

You could also make the boot in brown with tiny gold balls and mark lace holes with a no. 1 piping tube. Cut the zigzag top with sharp pointed scissors.

ELF BOOTS

Materials:

Mexican (flower/gum) paste in white
  and red

Tiny silver balls

Piping gel/edible glue

Tools:

Small non-stick rolling pin

1¼in (3cm) and 1½in (4cm)
  leaf/petal cutters

Multi-mould tiara

Music stave cutter

Dresden tool

Small sharp pointed scissors

Waterbrush/small paintbrush
  and water

Instructions:

1 Roll out the white paste to a thickness of ¹⁄₂₀in (1mm).
Cut out a 1¼in (3cm) leaf/petal shape for the sole.

2 Roll out the red paste thinly. Allow to dry slightly on
each side until the paste feels leathery. Cut out two 1½in
(4cm) leaf/petal shapes.

3 Dampen the sides of the sole. Attach the red leaf/petal
shapes to the sole, starting at the toe end, gently pressing
the paste carefully to the sides of the sole. Use the Dresden
tool to help shape the boot from the inside. Dampen the
heel end and along the top at the front and press together,
leaving the wide end open on top.

4 Make two white tiaras from the multi-mould using
white paste. Stick them around the top of the boot with
the points facing down.

5 Roll out the white paste thinly. Leave it to dry for a few
minutes until it feels leathery, turning it over occasionally.
Cut out a short strip using the music stave cutter. Dampen
a point a little way along the strip. Form a tiny loop and tail
by bringing the end over to the dampened point, press in
and bend the tail away from the loop. Repeat, bringing the
other end in to the same point to form another loop and
tail. Cut the tails to length using sharp pointed scissors.
Dampen the back of the boot to attach the bow.

6 Glue some tiny silver sugar balls to the point of the shoe
with a little piping gel or edible glue.

OWL

Materials:

Just under 1oz (25g) brown or chocolate fondant (sugarpaste)

Small amounts of white, pale brown and black fondant (sugarpaste)

Tools:

Small sharp-pointed scissors

Small sieve/sugarcraft gun

Heart cutter: 1in (2.5cm)

Circle cutters: ¾in (2cm) and ⅜in (1cm)

Small rolling pin

Instructions:

1 To make the beak, form a tiny cone from brown fondant (sugarpaste).

2 For the two wings, model each from a large pea-sized piece of brown paste and make into a fat carrot shape. Flatten slightly and mark on the feathers using the Dresden tool.

3 To make the body, roll the main piece of brown fondant (sugarpaste) into an oval shape, then roll it between your two fingers to form the neck and the head. Gently pinch and stroke the other end to form a short tail.

4 Cut out a heart from some thinly rolled-out white fondant (sugarpaste) and stick on the body for a tummy. Use fine sharp-pointed scissors (with points towards the feet of the owl) to snip through the surface of the paste on the tummy to form lots of little spikes. Stroke the spikes downwards to look like feathers. When snipping with the scissors the underneath colour will then show.

5 Attach the wings to the sides of the body.

6 To make the face, roll out white paste thinly. Cut out a ¾in (2cm) and a ⅜in (1cm) circle. Cut each circle into quarters, attach one of the larger quarters for the chin and

mark with the Dresden tool to suggest feathers. For the eye area, roll out some pale brown paste. Cut out a ¾in (2cm) circle and cut it into quarters. Stick two of the small white quarters to the pale brown ones. Stick on two small eyes made from two balls of black fondant (sugarpaste). Attach these two quarters and a plain quarter for the forehead, to the face. Mark the forehead with lines radiating outwards using the Dresden tool.

7 Attach the tiny brown beak.

8 Make two small pieces of white fluff by pressing some fondant (sugarpaste) through a sieve, sugarcraft gun, or garlic press. Stick it on to the head to look like the owl's ears.

Try using white fondant (sugarpaste) instead of chocolate or brown. When rolling out the paste for the tummy feathers, roll out white and pale brown, press together and roll again. Cut out the heart shape and stick to the tummy with the pale brown stuck to the body. When snipping with the scissors, the colour will then show.

RED GLITTER BAG

Materials:

- Red Mexican (flower/gum) paste
- Edible red glitter
- Piping gel

Tools:

- Small, non-stick rolling pin
- 1½in (4cm) square cutter
- ¼in (5mm) oval cutter
- Music stave cutter
- Fine stitching wheel
- Fine paintbrush

Instructions:

1 Roll the paste ⅛in (3mm) thick. Cut out two ¼in (5mm) ovals. Leave to dry.

2 Roll the paste thinly. Cut one 1½in (4cm) square and one strip using the music stave cutter.

3 Dampen along two sides of the square. Stand the ovals up on their ends about halfway down the sides of the square. Bring the bottom flap up over the edges of the ovals and then bring the top flap over to overlap the bottom flap.

4 Mark along the strip with the fine stitching wheel. Attach the ends to the sides of the bag.

5 For best results, allow the surface of the bag to dry before sticking the glitter on. Lay the bag on a piece of paper or plastic, so that the excess glitter can be poured back into the jar. Spread a thin layer of piping gel on the top flap of the bag. Sprinkle the edible glitter on to it. Use a dry paintbrush to brush away the excess glitter.

Cordelia is named after a Swedish friend, who made sure that the first Swedish word I learned was katt!

CORDELIA CAT

Materials:

²⁄₃oz (20g) cream
    modelling paste

2 x black sugar pearls

Tiny piece of brown
    fondant (sugarpaste)

Dark brown food
    colour powder

Vodka for painting

Small amount of blue
    fondant (sugarpaste)

Tools:

Dresden tool

Small paintbrush

Small, fine palette knife

Instructions:

1 Shape ¹⁄₆oz (5g) of modelling paste into a ball, mark two holes for the eyes using the Dresden tool and insert the black sugar pearl eyes.

2 Make two ears by shaping very small balls into pointed cone shapes and press the wide end of the Dresden tool in to make a dip in the middle. Dampen and attach them to the back of the head.

3 Make three very small balls of paste for the cheeks and chin and attach them to the face. Attach a tiny piece of brown fondant (sugarpaste) for the nose.

4 Cordelia's head is now complete.

5 Cut a ¹⁄₆oz (5g) piece of paste into four pieces, and shape the two back legs first by making two 1¼in (3cm) cones. Bend them in the middle and flatten the wide end slightly.

6 Shape the front legs into 1¼in (3cm) sausages and bend them in the middle. Mark three toes onto all four feet with the knife.

7 Shape the rest of the paste (about ¹⁄₃oz/10g) into a ball, then roll one end firmly to form the tail. Lengthen the body by rolling it in the palm of your hand. The overall length will be about 4in (10cm). Make it into a curved shape, then make a dip at the wide end for the head by pressing a finger in.

8 Dampen and attach both back legs, one leg under the body and one on top. Then attach both front legs.

9 Dampen the dip and attach the head to the body.

10 Shape the blue fondant (sugarpaste) into a rounded cone shape to make a tiny mouse and position it between Cordelia's paws.

11 Brush some dark brown food colour powder over Cordelia, avoiding her tummy and chin. Mix a little of the powder with a few drops of vodka, then paint on the markings.

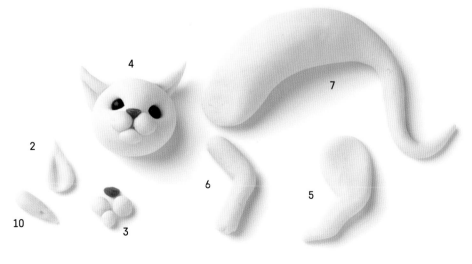

POLYMER CLAY KNOW-HOW

Pasta machine
To flatten the clay. A glass roller can also be used.

Aluminium foil
For creating armatures.

Scrap of lace or paper doily
For making impressions or decorations.

Polymer clay blocks
You will need a selection of standard 2oz (56g) blocks.

Materials and tools

The tools and techniques in this section have been kept to a minimum to ease the process for both novice and experienced modeller alike. Some of the tools listed can be substituted for everyday household implements; such as a glass tumbler instead of a roller, jar lids instead of cutters, cotton reels instead of embossing tools, and baking trays instead of ceramic tiles.

Wet wipes
For cleaning hands in between using different colours.

Oven thermometer
To ensure the clay is baked at the correct temperature.

Ceramic tile
To bake the polymer clay items on. You can also use a baking tray.

Polymer clay blade
For cutting clay.

Cookie cutters
For cutting out various shapes.

Blusher and brush
For adding colour to cheeks.

Knitting needle
To create eye sockets.

Wooden cocktail sticks
To create claws and folds.

Glass beads
For eyes.

Metal jump rings
For attaching charms, etc.

Other useful items

Acrylic paints and paintbrushes These are used to add coloured detail.

Varnish If you are using acrylic paint on the buttons (pages 226 and 238) then you will need to use varnish so that it does not come off when the items go through the washing machine. Nail polish is a good alternative.

Jump rings These are small metal rings used to press into the back of the buttons. They are usually used for jewellery making.

Cotton buds Small plastic rods with cotton wool on either end, these are used for applying colour with acrylic paints.

Embossing tools These are used to emboss the clay with interesting patterns. Common household items such as cotton reels are useful.

Proportions

These instructions are used to make the bears on pages 224 and 236.

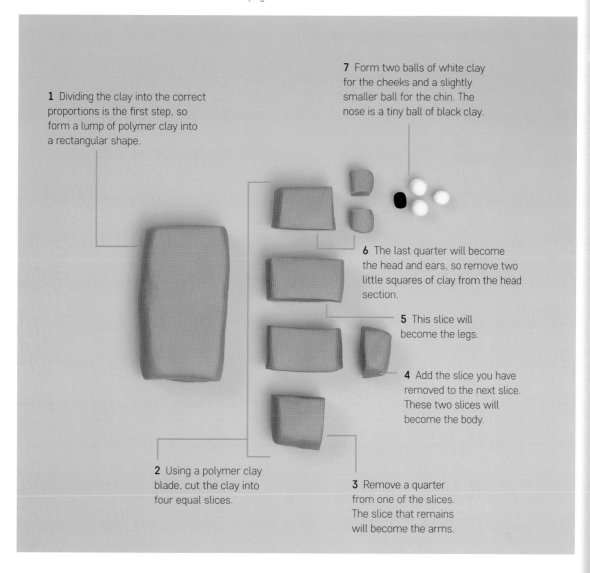

1 Dividing the clay into the correct proportions is the first step, so form a lump of polymer clay into a rectangular shape.

7 Form two balls of white clay for the cheeks and a slightly smaller ball for the chin. The nose is a tiny ball of black clay.

6 The last quarter will become the head and ears, so remove two little squares of clay from the head section.

5 This slice will become the legs.

4 Add the slice you have removed to the next slice. These two slices will become the body.

2 Using a polymer clay blade, cut the clay into four equal slices.

3 Remove a quarter from one of the slices. The slice that remains will become the arms.

Have a charming Christmas with this festive trinket! You can make three candy canes in different colours as an alternative.

CHRISTMAS CHARMS

Materials:

Polymer clay – brown, white, red, green and yellow

White paint

Strong glue

Varnish

Mini screw eyes

Jump rings

Chain

Lobster clasp

Ribbon

Tools:

Sandpaper

Rolling pin

Flower mini cutter or craft knife

Cocktail stick or modelling tool

Craft knife

Needle

Small sponge

Cutting pliers

Flat-nosed pliers

Brush for varnish

Instructions:

For all three pieces

Make a small hole in the top of each shape with a needle. Bake to set hard, following the instructions on the packet, then cool. Varnish. Fix mini screw eyes and jump rings. Attach the charms to chains with a clasp on the end.

Christmas pudding

1 Roll a 1in (2.5cm) ball of brown polymer clay. Roll it on some coarse sandpaper to give it a texture.

2 Flatten a small piece of white polymer clay to 1⁄32in (1mm) thick with a rolling pin. Cut the topping using a flower-shaped mini cutter or cut freehand with a craft knife.

3 Press the white topping on to the pudding. Add holly leaves cut from 1⁄32in (1mm) thick green polymer clay. Use a cocktail stick or modelling tool to mark the central lines of the holly leaves. Roll tiny red berries for a finishing touch.

Yule log

4 Flatten out 1¼in (3cm) diameter brown and yellow polymer clay balls to 1⁄8in (3mm) thick with a rolling pin. Cut both colours into 2⅜ x 1½in (6 x 4cm) rectangles.

5 Place the two pieces together with the yellow on top.

6 Roll the two colours together into a spiral. Keep rolling and stretching until you have a smooth cylinder ⅝in (1.5cm) in diameter. Cut off a 1in (2.5cm) length and add lines with a cocktail stick or modelling tool.

7 Make holly as for the Christmas pudding and bake it. Make a small hole in the top of the log with a needle and bake separately from the holly. Using a small sponge, apply a dusting of white paint over the log. Glue the holly leaves and berries on top.

Candy cane

8 Roll red and white polymer clay sausage shapes around 2⅜in (6cm) long and ¼in (5mm) in diameter.

9 Twist the two pieces together. Keep rolling and twisting until the stripes look the right distance apart, then cut off a 2in (5cm) length and shape into a candy cane.

10 Tie a small ribbon around the candy cane when baked and cooled.

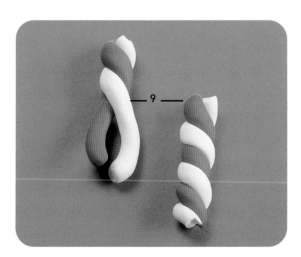
— 9 —

The Teddy Bear is shown here with two friends. The larger blue bear has a brown snout and a very big nose. He also has little brown matching pads on his paws, which are created by squashing tiny flattened balls of brown clay into place. He has larger ears and his eyes are closer together. The little pink bear has a tiny, round nose made from deep pink clay. Her ears have been placed further down and she holds a blanket made from flattened white clay. The claws were created using a cocktail stick to make the indentations.

TEDDY BEAR

Materials:

Half a block of brown polymer clay

A little white clay and a tiny spot of black
for the nose

Two tiny glass beads for eyes

Tools:

Polymer clay blade to cut the clay

Knitting needle to create the ear holes

Half a wooden cocktail stick to support the head

A cocktail stick to insert the glass beads

Ceramic tile or baking tray

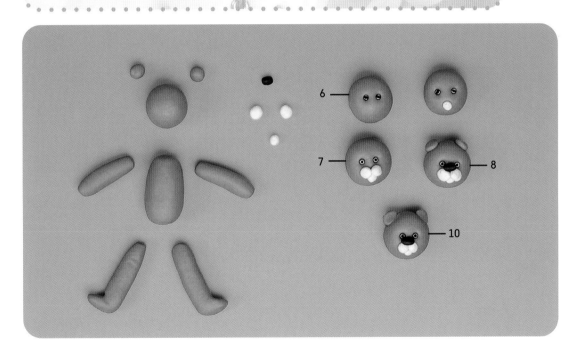

Instructions:

1 Divide the clay as shown on page 221.

2 Form the shapes as shown above.

3 Attach the legs to the body by pressing firmly, taking care not to distort the tops of the legs.

4 Attach the arms.

5 Push the blunt end of the half cocktail stick into the top of the body, leaving a little protruding, as shown (opposite).

6 Insert the glass beads as eyes, using the cocktail stick.

7 Add the chin followed by the cheeks as shown above.

8 Attach the little black nose.

9 Place the head firmly down on the protruding cocktail stick to attach it to the body.

10 To make the ears, press the little balls firmly on the head, then pinch them to flatten them slightly.

11 Use the knitting needle to create the ear holes.

12 Bake your bear at the recommended temperature on a ceramic tile or baking tray.

For a different look, try swapping the colours to a cool turquoise or cheerful yellow.

OWL BUTTON

Materials:

- Burgundy or dark red polymer clay blocks
- Small amount of pink polymer clay
- Tiny amounts of white and brown polymer clay
- Brown and white acrylic paint
- Varnish for the eyes and wings

Tools:

- Pasta machine or roller
- Polymer clay blade
- 1⅛in (30mm) circle cutter for the button
- ¾in (20mm) heart shaped or circle cutter
- Cocktail sticks
- Small soft paintbrush
- Ceramic tile or baking tray

Instructions:

1 Begin by softening the burgundy clay you need for your button, then roll it out using a pasta machine or roller. Your rolled out piece should be at least ⅛in (3mm) thick.

2 Using a 1⅛in (30mm) diameter circle cutter, cut out your shape.

3 To create the ears, pinch the top of the circle with your fingers while pulling upwards slightly.

4 For the eyes, take a small amount of white clay and roll it into two small ball shapes. Press down on each with your finger to flatten them. Make a criss cross design on the white circles using your blade (see detail).

5 Place these circles on to the owl, and in the centre of each, place a small amount of brown clay, flattened in the same way as the white parts of the eyes.

6 For the wings, roll out a small amount of pink clay. This should be around 1⁄16in (1mm) thick.

7 Using a smaller ¾in (20mm) diameter circle cutter or heart shape, cut out a shape from the pink clay and cut it in half with the blade. Place these two halves on to the owl as wings.

8 Use your blade to cut out a small triangle shape from the pink clay to create the beak. Place the beak on to the owl.

9 Before baking your owl, gently press down on all the pieces that you have attached to ensure they are firmly in place.

10 Make three holes in the centre of the button using a cocktail stick, slowly turning it as you push so you do not distort the shape. Place the button on to a ceramic tile and bake following the instructions on the clay packet.

11 Once your button is cool, use a cocktail stick dipped into dark brown acrylic paint to create the polka dots on the wings, and white acrylic paint for the highlight on the eyes.

12 When the acrylic paint has dried (this can take around thirty minutes) apply one coat of varnish to the wings and eyes using a small, soft paintbrush.

Add white 'icing' to gingerbread shapes made with mini cutters. Glue on tiny silver beads.

GINGERBREAD CHARMS

Materials:

Polymer clay – brown, white, red, green, yellow and lilac

Varnish

Mini screw eyes

Jump rings

Chain

Lobster clasp

Tools:

Paper

Scissors

Rolling pin

Craft knife and cutting mat

Garlic press

Needle

Brush for varnish

Cutting pliers

Flat-nosed pliers

Instructions:

1 Photocopy or trace the template shapes (right) on to paper and then cut them out.

2 Flatten some brown polymer clay with a rolling pin to 1¼in (3cm).

3 Carefully cut around the templates with a craft knife as shown below.

4 Remove the templates and smooth down the edges of the house, star and gingerbread man with your fingers.

5 Use the garlic press to make very thin strands of brighly coloured polymer clay, and also make tiny rolled balls. Decorate the shapes with the strands and balls.

6 Make a small hole in the top of each shape with a needle.

7 Bake all the shapes to set hard, then cool. Varnish.

8 Fix mini screw eyes into the holes then add jump rings on a chain with a lobster clasp.

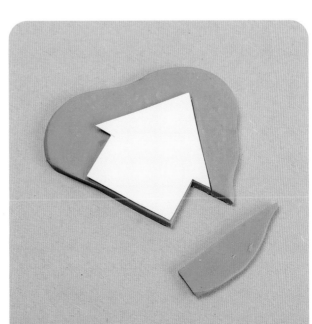

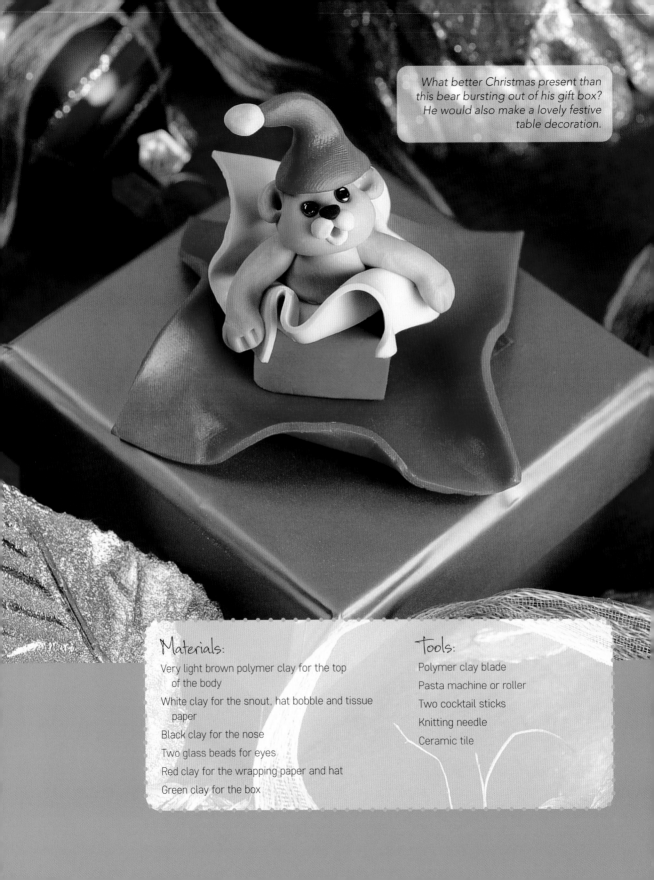

What better Christmas present than this bear bursting out of his gift box? He would also make a lovely festive table decoration.

Materials:

Very light brown polymer clay for the top of the body

White clay for the snout, hat bobble and tissue paper

Black clay for the nose

Two glass beads for eyes

Red clay for the wrapping paper and hat

Green clay for the box

Tools:

Polymer clay blade

Pasta machine or roller

Two cocktail sticks

Knitting needle

Ceramic tile

CHRISTMAS BEAR

Instructions:

1 Create the top half of a bear and arms from light brown clay.

2 Form the green polymer clay into a box shape.

3 Flatten the white clay and cut into a square. Form the white bobble ready for the hat.

4 Flatten the red clay and cut into a larger square.

5 For the hat, first create a ball of red clay, then place your thumb at the base and ease it into the hat shape shown above.

6 Place half a cocktail stick in the green box, with the point facing upwards.

7 Lay the box on top of the red sheet and fluff up the red sheet to resemble paper.

8 Place the white sheet over the cocktail stick and fluff this up too.

9 Place the assembled half-bear over the protruding point of the cocktail stick.

10 Add the hat and bobble and for a surprised expression, use the knitting needle to open his mouth.

11 Bake to set hard, following the manufacturer's instructions, then cool.

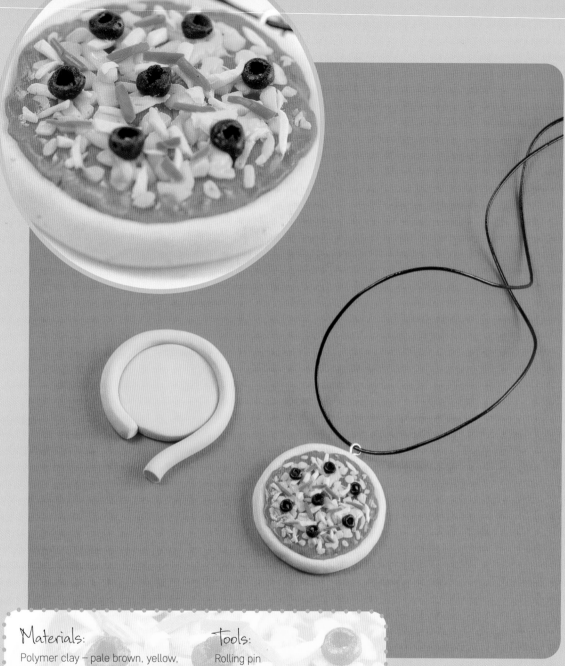

Materials:

Polymer clay – pale brown, yellow,
    red, green and black

Varnish

Mini screw eye

Cotton cord

Crimps

Jump rings

Clasp

Tools:

Rolling pin

1¼in (3cm) circle cutter or lid

Cocktail stick or modelling tool

Needle

Brush for varnish

Flat-nosed pliers

PIZZA NECKLACE

Instructions:

1 Roll out some pale brown polymer clay with a rolling pin to ¼in (5mm) thick. Cut a 1¼in (3cm) diameter circle using a cutter or circular lid.

2 Roll a sausage of pale brown polymer clay ¼in (5mm) in diameter x 4in (10cm) long. Carefully wrap it around the edge of the circle.

3 Roll some red polymer clay to ⅛in (2mm) thick. Cut out a 1¼in (3cm) diameter circle then press around the edges to make a slightly irregular shape.

4 Place the red piece on the pizza. Sprinkle tiny pieces of sliced yellow polymer clay on to the pizza for the cheese. Add some green pieces on top.

5 Roll minature balls of black polymer clay ⅛in (3mm) diameter for the olives. Push a cocktail stick through the middles to make holes, then add to the pizza.

6 Push a needle into the side of the pizza.

7 Bake to set hard then cool. Varnish.

8 Fix a mini screw eye into the hole, then thread a length of cotton cord through it. Attach crimps to the ends of the cord and add a jump ring on to one end and a clasp to the other.

233

For a charm bracelet, make the pizza base in the same way as for the necklace, with a yellow circle added to the inside instead of red, then cut it into six equal slices. Sprinkle on different coloured toppings. Use mini screw eyes to attach the charms to the bracelet chain.

MELON SLICE EARRINGS

Materials:

Polymer clay – red/pink mix, white,
  glittery green and black

Varnish

Mini screw eyes

Jump rings

Earring wires

Tools:

Rolling pin

Craft knife or polymer clay blade and
  cutting mat

Brush for varnish

Needle

Flat-nosed pliers

Instructions:

1 Roll a ¾in (2cm) diameter ball of blended red/pink polymer clay. Roll a 1in (2.5cm) ball of white polymer clay and use a rolling pin to flatten it to a ⅛in (2mm) thick circle.

2 Wrap the rolled white circle around the red ball. Cut away any folds so it is the same thickness all the way round. Roll it smooth.

3 Roll a 1¼in (3cm) diameter ball of glittery green polymer clay. Flatten it with a rolling pin into a circle shape ⅛in (2mm) thick.

4 Wrap the rolled glittery green circle around the white ball in the same way as before, cutting away any folds and rolling it smooth.

5 Use a polymer clay blade or an extended craft knife to carefully slice the ball in half, then cut off two wedge-shaped sections. Reshape each wedge if necessary.

6 Press tiny black polymer clay 'seeds' on both sides of the wedges. Make a small hole in the top of each piece with a needle.

7 Bake to set hard, following the instructions on the packet, then cool. Varnish and leave to dry.

8 Fix mini screw eyes into each piece of melon. Add jump rings and earring wires.

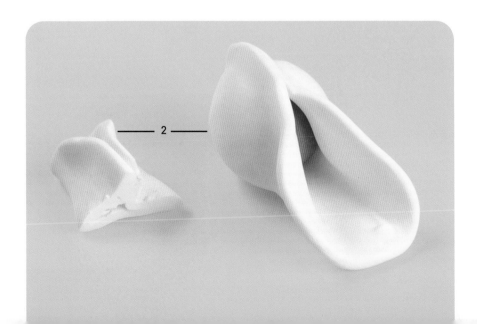

The other polar bear is sitting up, making snowballs. A little blusher applied to his face adds a touch of life.

POLAR BEAR

Materials:

Half a block of white
  polymer clay
A little black clay
Two glass beads for eyes
Blusher (optional)

Tools:

Polymer clay blade
Cocktail sticks
Knitting needle
Ceramic tile

Instructions:

1 Divide the clay as shown on page 221. The body needs to be shaped slightly longer than the bear on page 225. It also needs a little stump of a tail.

2 Form the shapes for the body and the back and front legs as shown below. Insert the half cocktail stick ready to support the head.

3 Attach the front and back legs.

4 Form a ball for the head, then create two eye sockets using the knitting needle. Insert two tiny balls of white clay into each, then add the glass beads.

5 The snout is created out of two lumps of white clay. For the top part, form a short, fat white sausage shape. Push it firmly on to the head.

6 Use a cocktail stick to create a vertical crease, then add a smaller ball of clay beneath it to form a mouth.

7 Add a nice big, black nose and little white ears.

8 Attach the head to the body and bake on a ceramic tile or baking tray until hard, following the instructions on the packet. Allow to cool.

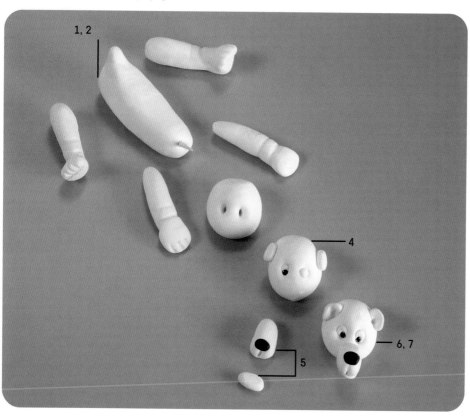

Decorate your cupcake buttons by using tiny beads on the frosting. You can also use a larger bead or polymer clay flower in place of the polymer clay cherry.

CUPCAKE BUTTON

Materials:

Red and white polymer clay

White acrylic paint

Varnish

Tools:

Pasta machine or roller

Polymer clay blade

Cocktail stick

Jump ring

Ceramic tile or baking tray

Soft and fine paintbrushes

Instructions:

1 Roll out the red clay, using a pasta machine or roller, to around ⅛in (3mm) thickness.

2 Cut out a ¾in (20mm) square from the sheet of red clay using your blade. Cut off the edges of the red square with your blade to make a cupcake case shape as shown.

3 Make the ridges on the cupcake case piece by pressing the length of a cocktail stick firmly into the clay (see detail).

4 Roll some white clay into a sausage shape and cut it into three different size pieces, one ¾in (20mm), one ½in (12mm) and one ¼in (7mm) in length. Put the icing together by laying the longest piece at the bottom and the shortest piece on the top.

5 Use a cocktail stick to create the ridges on the icing piece by pressing the side of it in (see detail).

6 For the cherry, roll a small amount of red clay into a ball.

7 Attach all the pieces together.

8 Press a jump ring into the back of your cupcake. To make sure the jump ring stays in your button, press a tiny

amount of clay through the jump ring and press down firmly.

9 Place your cupcake on to a ceramic tile and bake until hard, following the instructions on the packet.

10 Once your button has completely cooled, take a cocktail stick and dip the tip into a small amount of white acrylic paint. Touch it to the cupcake case part to create a polka dot design. Use a fine paintbrush to paint a highlight on the cherry.

11 Once the acrylic paint has dried, use the soft paintbrush to apply one coat of varnish to the polka dotted areas and to the cherry.

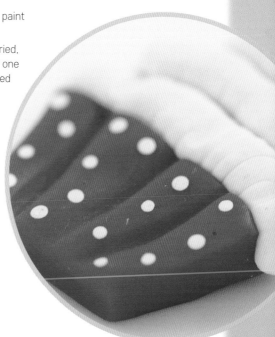

Quick and Easy Christmas uses material from the following books in the *Twenty to Make* series published by Search Press:

Stitching
Bunting and Pennants by Kate Haxell, 2011
Fabric Flowers by Kate Haxell, 2011
Needle Felties by Susanna Wallis, 2012
Mini Bunting by Alistair Macdonald, 2013
Felt Christmas Decorations by Corinne Lapierre, 2013
Mini Cross Stitch by Michael Powell, 2013
Jelly Roll Scraps by Carolyn Forster, 2013
Stitched Fabric Brooches by Alex McQuade, 2014
Felt Brooches with Free-machine Stitching by Myra Hutton, 2014
Fabulous Pompoms by Alistair Macdonald, 2014
Pompom Christmas by Alistair Macdonald, 2015
Faux Fur Fun by Alistair Macdonald, 2015
Silk Ribbon Flowers by Ann Cox, 2015
Modern Needlepoint by Jayne Schofield, 2016

Papercraft
Tags and Toppers by Michelle Powell, 2008
Mini Gift Boxes by Michelle Powell, 2009
Washi Tape Cards by Sara Naumann, 2014
Quilled Animals by Diane Boden, 2014
Modern Decoupage by Louise Crosbie, 2015
Papercuts by Paper Panda, 2015

Knitting
Knitted Cakes by Susan Penny, 2008
Knitted Bears by Val Pierce, 2009
Knitted Flowers by Susie Johns, 2009
Knitted Mug Hugs by Val Pierce, 2010
Mini Christmas Knits by Sue Stratford, 2011
Knitted Vegetables by Susie Johns, 2011
Knitted Baby Bootees by Val Pierce, 2011
Knitted Fruit by Susie Johns, 2011
Knitted Beanies by Susie Johns, 2012
Knitted Boot Cuffs by Monica Russel, 2012
Knitted Phone Sox by Susan A. Cordes, 2013
Easy Knitted Scarves by Monica Russel, 2013
Knitted Wrist Warmers by Monica Russel, 2014
Easy Knitted Tea Cosies by Lee Ann Garrett, 2014
Knitted Headbands by Monica Russel, 2015

Jewellery
Bracelets by Amanda Walker, 2007
Charms by Stephanie Burnham, 2007
Necklaces by Stephanie Burnham, 2008
Tiaras and Hairpins by Michelle Bungay, 2008
Beaded Felt Jewellery by Helen Birmingham, 2008
Celtic Jewellery by Amanda Walker, 2010
Button Jewellery by Marrianne Mercer, 2011
Pewter Jewellery by Sandy Griffiths, 2014
Modern Friendship Bracelets by Pam Leach, 2014
Steampunk Jewellery by Carolyn Schulz, 2014
Leather Jewellery by Natalia Colman, 2015
Simple Statement Rings by Carolyn Schulz, 2015

Crochet
Crocheted Bears by Val Pierce, 2011
Mini Christmas Crochet by Val Pierce, 2011
Crocheted Flowers by Jan Ollis, 2011
Crocheted Granny Squares by Val Pierce, 2012
Crocheted Beanies by Frauke Kiedaisch, 2013
Crocheted Hearts by May Corfield, 2015
Crocheted Purses by Anna Nikipirowicz, 2015
Granny Square Flowers by May Corfield, 2016

Sugarcraft
Sugar Animals by Frances McNaughton, 2009
Sugar Flowers by Lisa Slatter, 2011
Sugar Birds by Frances McNaughton, 2011
Mini Sugar Shoes by Frances McNaughton, 2012
Mini Sugar Bags by Frances McNaughton, 2013
Sugar Fairies by Frances McNaughton, 2013
Sugar Wobblies by Georgie Godbold, 2013
Sugar Scaries by Frances McNaughton, 2013
Sugar Christmas Decorations by Georgie Godbold, 2014
Sugar Dogs by Frances McNaughton, 2014
Sugar Cats by Frances McNaughton, 2015

Polymer Clay
Tasty Trinkets by Charlotte Stowell, 2010
Polymer Clay Bears by Birdy Heywood, 2010
Polymer Clay Buttons by Karen Walker, 2013

SEARCH PRESS LIMITED
The world's finest art and craft books

For all our books and catalogues go to **www.searchpress.com**

Follow us @searchpress on: